pretty delicious

Lean and Lovely Recipes for a Healthy, Happy New You

Candice Kumai

Photographs by Quentin Bacon

RODALE

Rodale books may be purchased for business or promotional use or for special sales. For information, please write to: Special Markets Department, Rodale Inc., 733 Third Avenue, New York, NY 10017.

Printed in the United States of America

Rodale Inc. makes every effort to use acid-free ♾, recycled paper ♻.

Book design by Kara Plikaitis

Prop Styling by Natasha Louise King

Library of Congress Cataloging-in-Publication Data

Kumai, Candice.
    Pretty delicious : lean and lovely recipes for a healthy, happy new you / Candice Kumai.
        p.   cm.
    Includes index.
    ISBN 978-1-60529-350-9 (hardcover)
    1. Low-calorie diet—Recipes. I. Title.
  RM222.2.K857 2010
  641.5′635—dc22

2010030188

Distributed to the trade by Macmillan

  4 6 8 10 9 7 5 3   hardcover

www.rodalebooks.com

Mom, you taught me how to share my love
thru clothing and to dream in creativity.
Dad, you showed me where integrity, hard
work & good faith would get me.
Sis, you remind me to be real, to give
back and to always just be new.

I love you all, my heart doesn't
even have the words.
Thank you. ♥ KC

Contents

Introduction

These days it seems like everyone is trying to tighten their belts—financially and literally. The problem is that too many of us fall into the weight loss marketing trap: paying lots of cash for processed, packaged "diet" food that's loaded with junk, from artificial colors and flavors to nasty preservatives. Crash diets, starvation, and fake food (yes, that's "fake food," as in made in a science lab!) loaded with fillers and chemicals aren't the solution to looking fabulous forever. In fact, oftentimes we're making ourselves sick (and broke!) from chemicals and additives when we're trying to make ourselves healthier! And what's sadder than eating dinner out of a microwave tray? I want fresh, seasonal foods that are beautiful on the plate—and that I've chosen myself.

So I came up with an easy philosophy for eating well that's healthy, lean, *and* budget friendly. Instead of filling up on things I know I shouldn't be eating, like processed foods, empty carbs, and unwanted sat fats, I pack my menus with what I call FWBs—Foods with Benefits. I don't deny myself anything (check out the dessert chapter if you have any doubts on that score), but by building every meal around my fave FWBs, the good stuff naturally takes center stage, while the stuff that should be eaten in moderation gets pushed into the wings in a supporting role. The result is *real* food that doesn't cost an arm and a leg, is simple to prepare, and makes you gorgeous inside and out.

Cooking with FWBs is all about eating food to benefit your body. For example, quinoa is a seed that cooks up like couscous but delivers a heaping helping of essential amino acids (the building blocks of protein) and filling fiber. So why eat couscous when you can eat quinoa? While you're at it, how about swapping vitamins A- and C-packed oven-baked sweet potato fries for the greasy, fat-loaded fries you sneak every now and then?

The first step is simple. Just go to the store and make an investment in whole, natural, unprocessed foods. Organic is great if you can get it—and yes, it IS worth the added expense for both your health and that of the planet—and farmers' markets have wonderfully fresh foods from local farms and producers. But even if you do all your food shopping at the local megamarket, just by chosing real, whole foods you'll be that much closer to a more gorgeous, happier, and healthier you.

My new outlook on food began when I realized my approach to "diet" just wasn't working for me. You see, I was paid to have the perfect body because I was a fit model. That meant I had to maintain a 26-inch waist, 35-inch hips, and 20-inch thighs on the money, no ifs, ands, or butts about it. Most days I got through the day on an endless stream of Diet Coke and an occasional handful of nuts (okay, I sometimes splurged on a sugar-monster frappuccino!). But it always felt wrong to me, and by the time I was 23 (a dinosaur in the modeling world) I realized that kind of

$$$ Skinny Waist, Fat Wallet? Totally!

I quickly learned that pinching pennies is as easy as pinching pounds—it just takes a little planning and a lot of ingenuity. I've loaded the book with tons of tips and ideas for stretching your budget without blowing your diet. One trick is to shop seasonally, as seasonal produce is most often less expensive than the stuff flown in from abroad or trucked cross-country. Another is to keep an eye out for sales on your favorite protein foods—when the price is right, stock up and freeze for a later meal. Shopping generic for foods is a good practice too, as most often generic products are exactly the same as the brand name ones! Don't believe me? Just read the labels. And when you *do* read the labels, pay attention not only to calories, carbs, and fat grams, but to sodium as well. Once you see what you're really paying for you'll realize that making food from scratch always beats processed and packaged—from homemade barbecue sauce (page 176) to salad dressings, marinades, and to-die-for hummus (page 49)—whether you're looking out for your health *or* your wallet.

Cooking amazing, healthy food on a slim budget has never been tastier, and soon you'll not only look and feel better than ever, but you'll want to invite your friends over to share in the fabulousness. I don't know what I'd do without my girlfriends—entertaining is a part of my life that I refuse to give up, even if I only have $10 to make dinner! That's why I've included tons of party-friendly, chic, and modern recipes that won't leave you in the poorhouse afterward.

diet just wasn't getting the job done. Plus, I missed eating the kind of delicious, flavorful, REAL food I'd grown up on.

My mom is Japanese and my dad is Polish-American, so our dinner table was always a crazy cultural mix. I don't know many people who count both miso soup and pierogis among their fave comfort foods! But it was all made with care, with the best ingredients we could afford, and it was always homemade. Throughout my childhood, my mom cooked dinner every night (she'd often have to come and drag me in from the sandbox where I'd be playing "cooking show" with old melamine dishes) and packed me the best brown-bag lunches my school had ever seen.

When I finally decided I couldn't deny my love of food any longer, I did a complete 180 and went to culinary school. I learned the basics in Le Cordon Bleu College of Culinary Arts in Los Angeles and found myself becoming passionate, studious, and serious about something other than surfing or Betsey Johnson for the first time in my life! My classmates loved to tease me about the fact that I traded my Manolos for chef clogs when I came through the kitchen (that's how I earned my nickname the "Stiletto Chef"). But even though peeling potatoes and carrots for $6 an hour was a far cry from earning $150 an hour for trying on jeans, I knew I had found my true calling.

I also had a rude awakening. After years of denial and dieting, I gained 10 pounds during my two terms of baking. With my tuition due and the realities of a chef's tiny starting salary staring me in the face, I knew I had to raise cash fast, which meant getting back into modeling (and my jeans!). I had to teach myself about balance and moderation—and pronto.

Fortunately it didn't take me long to figure out how to trim a few fat grams and calories here and there while still eating great and keeping healthy and sexy once I really put my mind to it. I became the queen of swapping (not sacrificing), but always with flavor leading the way. Before long I had a collection of recipes that tasted great and were great for me too. Not bad for a surfer-girl-turned-model-turned-chef, right?

Baker

After getting pulled out of culinary school to compete on the first season of Bravo's *Top Chef*, I did stints at upscale restaurant kitchens and then was cast as a host for Lifetime's *Cook Yourself Thin*, a cooking show that really allowed me to make a difference in people's lives. I went on to do more shows on Lifetime and the Cooking Channel. It was amazing and gratifying to see the pounds lost by people who had successfully followed my approach to healthy eating. It seemed I wasn't the only one who needed to make some big changes in her diet, and it was exciting to be a part of that change.

One refrain (excuse?) I heard time and again was that eating healthy just seemed so expensive. But I promise to keep you feeling healthy, looking fabulous, and eating great—all for less money than you'd think! It's really all about making good choices, and thinking about every single thing you do—and don't—put on your plate.

When I create a recipe I always ask myself "What health benefits am I getting from the food I am putting into my body?" If I'm dishing up glazed salmon with Swiss chard, then I know I'm getting omega-3s, protein, and good monounsaturated fats from the fish and filling fiber and vitamins A, C, and K from the chard. If the answer is "Not much," then I know it's something I should eat in moderation or as an occasional treat (that's where my Chocolate-Peanut Butter Crunch Cups come in!). That's why my recipes tell you exactly which FWBs you'll be getting from each, and when you need to keep the intake turned to low. Thinking of food as the gas your body runs on will help you make better choices every day, especially when you have a plethora of delicious, fresh, easy, and economical choices like these to choose from. This is simply how I eat, cook, and think about food. With moderation and not deprivation, you can get sexy, gorgeous, and healthy and stay that way forever!

look it's me!

P.S. For more delish recipes and crafty fun, visit me at www.stilettochef.com.

7 Slimming Ways to Stretch Food and Save Calories and Cash!

From a young age I've been a penny wise kind of girl, and I have to thank Mom for that. She was my great Kumai *sensei*! Now it's my turn to share these time-honored tricks and tips with you. Put them to use to transfer padding from your hips to your bank account!

1. **Make your own dressings, marinades, and sauces.**
   Since you control what's going into them, you can keep the bad junk out. Check out my Skinny 'Cue Sauce (page 176) and 2-Second Honey-Mustard (page 20) for starters. Pan sauces made after searing meat are a great way to use up leftover wine, too!

2. Boost ground meat with veggies.

Adding sautéed mushrooms, peppers, onions, fresh corn, and even beans to ground meat before making burgers, meatballs, or meat loaf adds vitamins and nutrients and reduces fat. Plus, it stretches your meat so you can feed more people for the same price.

3. Re-think your plate.

Fill at least half of your plate with fresh veggies (seasonal veggies are often cheaper than those flown and trucked in from afar—so go for zucchini and peppers in the summer and squash and root veggies in the winter) and trim the protein down to one-quarter of the plate. Whole grains like quinoa or brown rice can make up the remaining one-quarter.

4. Don't let leftovers go to waste.

Or think of it this way: Every time you throw out food, you might as well be throwing your hard-earned dinero in the trash! Burritos, stir-fries, lasagna, sandwiches, soups, chilis, and omelets are all great uses for leftover chicken, beef, vegetables, and rice.

5. Go "ovo" board for dinner.

Why not eat eggs for dinner? They're a lean and inexpensive way to work in your protein. Frittatas, omelets, or a veggie sandwich topped with hard-cooked egg slices are all smart ways to go.

6. You "can" afford fish.

If fresh fish is out of your price range, go for canned. Salmon, tuna, and sardines are all super healthy and delicious, and much cheaper than their fresh friends.

7. It's a breeze when you freeze.

After making dinner, get into the habit of freezing leftovers right away. Preportion them in single-serving sizes, which are perfect when it comes to brown-bagging a lunch or when you need a meal in a pinch. Breads and tortillas also can be frozen—just be sure to wrap them in a double layer of plastic wrap and store them in resealable freezer bags to ward off freezer burn (use them within 2 to 3 months for the freshest flavor).

The FWB Philosophy

It took me 10 long years to figure out that a meal full of fake ingredients, even if it is low in fat and calories, isn't healthy. Whether you're into fat-free, low-cal, no-carb, all-protein, or fasting, the bottom line is this: Food is going to be around for the rest of your life, so you might as well learn to make peace with it. Instead of stuffing yourself with fake food created in chem labs, why not learn to eat what benefits your bod, mind, and spirit?

That's what eating Foods with Benefits (FWBs) is all about—keeping your diet simple and real. That means real food, real ingredients, like veggies, lean proteins, tofu, whole grains, nuts, fruit, and yes, even bittersweet chocolate! Throughout *Pretty Delicious* I've highlighted the FWBs so you know exactly what you're getting out of the food going into your body. It's your choice. You can listen to the marketing monsters out there, the ones who try to sell us every diet fad, pill, shake, and nutzo plan, or you can opt out of the multibillion-dollar industry and just eat really good food. These are my go-to's. Also check out the chart on page xxiii for a detailed listing of common FWBs and the specific nutritional benefits of each.

* Antioxidant Powerhouses: Go ahead, say yes!
  Dark chocolate, red wine
* Babe-a-licious Berries: Small, but with a big impact
  Blueberries, dried cranberries, raspberries, strawberries
* Beans and Legumes: Cheap, fiber-ful, and fabulous
  Black beans, edamame, chickpeas, green beans, kidney beans
* Dairy and Un-Dairy: Beautiful bones
  Almond milk, nonfat Greek yogurt, cheese (especially reduced-fat)
* Fab Fruits: Nature's own fast food
  Apples, bananas, lemons, nectarines, pears, peaches
* Good Fats: A small bit does a whole lot of good
  Almonds, avocados, extra-virgin olive oil, flaxseeds, peanut butter, walnuts, salmon
* Healing Herbs and Sexy Spices: A flavor and health punch
  Basil, cilantro, cinnamon, coriander, cumin, curry powder, fresh and ground ginger, nutmeg, parsley
* Leafy Greens: Go green for life
  Arugula, collards/mustard greens, romaine, spinach, Swiss chard, watercress

❦ Lean Protein: Portion size is key—a deck of cards will do ya
  Chicken breast, eggs, lean beef, lean deli meat, mahi-mahi, shrimp, tofu, tuna

❦ Marvelous Mushrooms: Magic for your mind and body
  Cremini mushrooms, shiitake mushrooms, button mushrooms

❦ Totally Roots and Tubers: An underground sensation
  Beets, carrots, potatoes, sweet potatoes, parsnips

❦ Vibrant Veggies: Like grandma said . . . eat your veggies
  Artichokes, asparagus, bok choy, cabbage, cucumbers, eggplant, garlic, onions, pumpkin, red bell peppers, scallions, tomatoes, zucchini

❦ Whole Grains and Seeds: Plant a seed for your future
  Barley, brown rice, flaxseeds, oats, quinoa, wheat bran, whole wheat bread

Three Rules to Cook by

Think about your grandma (or great-grandma!). She cooked her own food, drank in moderation, worked hard, and didn't spend hours on her butt watching TV or parked in front of a computer screen. She didn't waste her money on processed food—she kept it real, fresh, healthy, and fabulous!

The lesson is: Eat junk, you get junk in the trunk. Eat fresh and fabulous and guess what? You're looking pretty fabulous. It's really a no-brainer. So get real, eat real, and start cooking real food. Here are my rules.

1. **You are what you eat.** Ask yourself before eating: What are the health benefits of this meal? What am I getting out of it? If it's a bag of chips, chances are you're getting empty calories and jiggly arms! Just say no! Always eat foods that give you bennies—hey, even chocolate has antioxidants!

2. **Think outside the box.** If you're buying something packaged, chances are it's junk food to begin with. Just because something has a shiny label that touts it as "healthy" or a "sensible solution" doesn't mean it isn't full of chemicals and other stuff you'd simply be better off not eating. And don't think that just because there are only 100 calories in the package it can't be that bad—after all, isn't that still 100 calories' worth of chemicals and junk? It comes down to this: You just can't go wrong chosing real, wholesome food over fillers, modified sugars and starches, and multisyllabic ingredients. If you can't pronounce it, assume it's not good for you!

3. Cookin' it old school. By now we know that diets suck, they don't work, and they're torture. It's time to go back to basics. Grandma didn't order a 20-piece bucket of fried chicken on the weekend, she cooked! Get back in your kitchen and stop protesting "I don't have time," or "cooking is too expensive." Throw your excuses in the excuse bin. Get your butt off of fast food and diet food and get into real food, old school, good cookin', good lookin'!

Tips for Staying Slim and Rich!

1. Buy food that does double duty and offers more than one health benefit. Nonfat Greek yogurt has calcium and protein—stock up. (Choose the containers with the latest "use by" dates if you're buying in bulk.) Potato chips have zero health benefits—leave them on the shelf!

2. Take charge of shopping. Shop with a list, buy sale items in bulk, and read those grocery flyers. Don't shop hungry or when you're super emo.

3. Stay away from the middle of the grocery store—that's where all that monster junk food is! Your safest bet? The farmers' market. Check out localharvest. org for a listing of farmers' markets near you.

4. Drink H_2O. I love fizzy mineral water. It keeps me fuller longer and comes in all kinds of flavors (make sure the kind you buy doesn't add artificial sweeteners or flavors). Or, make your own calorie-free spa water by adding cucumber slices, lemon wheels, cantaloupe or watermelon chunks, or fresh herbs.

5. Get moving. I try to do something active for at least 30 minutes every day. Some of my faves are freebies, too (no gym needed!), like a walk with a girlfriend, going to the dog park, gardening, cleaning (yes, you do burn calories cleaning!), doing an aerobics video with a friend, mowing the lawn, shooting hoops, or going for a swim.

6. Calories do count. What's your target weight? Add a zero and that's how many calories you should be eating a day. Keep track of how many calories you consume; numbers don't lie, and neither will those jeans.

7. Let yourself relax. When I'm feeling run down, I recharge by getting in some extra sleep or chilling with a good book. Rest is critical for a happy, healthy body.

8. Most important: Stay motivated, happy, and positive! Nothing brings more success your way than a great outlook on life. You're hot and you know it!

Some Final Food for Thought: 3 Steps to Skinny Success

This book isn't a program you need to follow meal by meal because, frankly, I think that's where we all trip up when it comes to eating well. As soon as we have someone telling us what to eat when, it feels too restrictive, and we rebel—and wind up on the couch surrounded by fast-food bags and candy wrappers. Ultimately it's about thinking about everything we put in our body and making better choices. Here's my philosophy.

1. **Diets suck**. They don't work. They are fake and cruel. They are simply a ploy to try to get you to spend money on gimmicks that fall short. No diet pill, power-up bar, chalky shake, preportioned dinner, or processed frozen meal is magically going to make you over. To get really healthy, you've got to get real. Take charge of your food, know how to separate the good from the bad, and change your lifestyle, honey.

2. **When lifestyle changes are realistic, they DO work!** Why embarrass yourself by weighing yourself in front of a bunch of strangers? In the privacy of your own home, on your own time, and in your own cute kitchen, you can become the mastermind of a plan to regain your skinny little waist. Cook healthy food, rein in your portions, and stay positive about yourself. You can do this—you *can* lose weight without shelling out your hard-earned cash to groups, clubs, and systems. Read what to splurge on and what to say sayonara to. Read the Frugal & Fab tips and Slim Scoops. If you slip up, no worries, just open this book up to a recipe that looks too good to be true, cook it, love it. Empowering yourself is the first step to a gorgeous you!

3. **You have the control.** Remember that the choices are yours to make; just let what's good for your well-being be your guide, and nothing else. Make a conscious decision to purchase better foods (no sugary bottled dressings, no cheese puffs!) and cook meals at home. The impact on your life, your bod, and your wallet will be huge. You *can* have it all. The skinny jeans, the fat bank account, the delicious food. It's all up to you!

Take action today. Clean out your fridge and pantry. Shop at the market with your goals firmly front and center. Think about the swimsuit for the cruise, or that slinky red dress for the reunion, and envision yourself looking like the ultimate dreamboat that you are. Get that sexy back, one meal at a time!

A final note: While I am happily omnivorous, like many people I am eating a lot less meat these days than I once did. For those of you who don't eat meat or would like to reduce the presence of meat in your diet, I have labeled vegetarian recipes (Ⓥ). For my vegan friends, recipes marked Ⓥ will be right up your alley!

FWB Forever!

The following list of my favorite Foods with Benefits is a great reference for learning more about what each food can offer you. I try to incorporate at least one FWB into every meal of the day. It's easy once you get the hang of it, and your strong, healthy, lean body will thank you!

(Please consult your doctor before starting any new health program or with any questions regarding a change in your diet.)

FWB	KEY NUTRIENTS	BENEFITS
Antioxidant Powerhouses		
Cocoa/dark chocolate	Antioxidants, flavonoids	Aids in cardiovascular health; may aid in anti-aging
Antiaging		
Red wine	Antioxidants, flavonoids, such as resveratrol	May aid in heart health
Babe-a-licious Berries		
Blueberries	Antioxidants, such as vitamin C	Vibrant eyes, healthy brain, great skin, major power food that could aid in the prevention of cancer
Cranberries	Antioxidants, such as vitamins C, K; fiber	Beautiful eyes
Raspberries	Antioxidants, such as vitamin C; calcium; folate	Great for the liver, muscles, and blood; help keep eyes and skin healthy
Strawberries	Antioxidants, such as vitamin C	Vibrant eyes; lower cholesterol levels; aid in healthy skin; may aid in the prevention of cancer
Beautiful Beans		
Black beans	Fiber, protein, folate, thiamin	Help lower blood pressure; aid in digestion; pack in energy
Edamame	Fiber, protein, folate, manganese	Great source of cholesterol-lowering fiber; aid in digestion; help stabilize blood sugar levels
Chickpeas (garbanzo beans)	Fiber, protein, folate, manganese	Great source of cholesterol-lowering fiber; aid in digestion; help stabilize blood sugar levels

FWB	KEY NUTRIENTS	BENEFITS
Beans—*Continued*		
Green beans	Vitamins A, C, and K; fiber; potassium	Lower blood pressure; keep bones healthy; aid in cardio health
Kidney beans	Fiber, protein, folate, manganese	Aid in digestion; help lower cholesterol; help stabilize blood sugar levels
Dairy and Nondairy		
Almond milk	Vitamins D and E; iron; phosphorus; calcium	Beautiful hair, skin, and nails; easily digested; low in calories
Nonfat Greek yogurt	Protein, calcium, vitamin D	Gorgeous hair, skin, and nails; strong bones; flat belly
Cheese	Calcium, protein	Sexy hair, nails, skin, and teeth
Fab Fruits		
Apples	Fiber; antioxidants, such as vitamin C	Healthy heart and cardiovascular benefits; aid in digestion
Bananas	Potassium; folate, niacin, thiamin; vitamins C, B_6, K	Help maintain alkali balance; contain good bacteria for a healthy tummy
Lemons	Vitamin C, fiber, calcium, iron	Boost immunity; aid in preventing heart disease and cancer
Nectarines	Beta-carotene, vitamin C, potassium, fiber	Vibrant eyes; healthy immune system
Peaches	Beta-carotene, vitamin C, potassium, fiber	Healthy immune system; vibrant eyes
Good Fats		
Almonds	Vitamin E, manganese, selenium	Help lower the risk of heart disease; may help lower cholesterol; great for supple skin and glowing complexion
Avocados	Vitamins A, C, and E; monoun-saturated ("good") fats	Beautiful hair, nails, and skin
Extra-virgin olive oil	Monounsaturated ("good") fats	Healthy hair, nails, and skin; may help with longevity; may help prevent heart disease; aids in lowering cholesterol

FWB	KEY NUTRIENTS	BENEFITS
Good Fats—*Continued*		
Peanut butter	Protein, fiber, vitamin E, resveratrol	Healthy plant protein; helps reduce risk of heart disease; helps maintain weight control
Walnuts	Omega-3s	Boost brain and heart health; good skin; help minimize premature aging and wrinkles; mood booster; decrease appetite
Healing Herbs and Sexy Spices		
Basil	Vitamins A and K; iron; flavonoids	Great for cardio health; natural antibiotic and anti-inflammatory properties; aids in digestion
Cilantro	Fiber, manganese, iron, flavonoids	Aids in digestion; prevents nausea; relieves intestinal discomfort; lowers blood sugar levels and cholesterol
Cinnamon	Manganese, fiber, iron, calcium	Fragrance may boost cognitive function and memory; improves colon health; antiseptic properties; aids digestion; good for the heart
Coriander	Fiber, iron, manganese, magnesium	Aids intestinal health; protects against infections; lowers bad cholesterol
Cumin	Iron, magnesium	Helps boost immunity; boosts energy; may aid in cancer prevention; aids in prenatal health and blood health
Curry powder	Vitamins B_6 and E; calcium; iron; zinc	Great for joint health; helps prevent Alzheimer's by improving memory; anti-inflammatory
Fresh and ground ginger	Vitamin B_6, potassium, magnesium	Immunity booster; helps relieve symptoms of nausea and headaches; anti-inflammatory; may help fight cancer
Nutmeg	Iron, calcium	Increases blood circulation; natural anti-inflammatory; may help curb appetite
Parsley	Antioxidants, such as vitamins A, C, and K; folate; iron	Healthy heart; fresh breath; aids in digestion; strong diuretic properties

FWB	KEY NUTRIENTS	BENEFITS
Leafy Greens		
Arugula	Vitamins A and C; folate; magnesium	Natural aphrodisiac properties; keeps eyes bright and body in good health
Collards/mustard greens	Vitamins A, C, and K; folate	Bright eyes; healthy lungs; vibrant skin
Romaine	Vitamins A, C, and K	Bright eyes; healthy heart; aids in digestion
Spinach	Folate; iron; riboflavin; thiamin; vitamins A, C, K, and B_6	Strong bones; healthy heart; may help prevent cancer
Swiss chard	Vitamins A, C, E, and K; potassium; iron; fiber	Beautiful eyes; clear skin
Watercress	Vitamins C, E, and K; beta-carotene; antioxidants	Healthy, clear skin
Lean Protein		
Chicken breasts	Niacin, vitamin B_6, protein	Lean muscles; healthy skin and bones
Eggs	Protein; riboflavin; vitamins A, B_{12}, B_6, and D; iron; calcium	Healthy teeth and bones; vibrant eyes; major brain booster; protein for muscles
Lean beef	Protein; riboflavin; niacin; vitamins B_6 and B_{12}; zinc; iron	Helps with emotional and mental well-being; brain booster; healthy red blood cells; energy; aids in cardio health
Lean deli meat	Protein	Lean muscles; healthy and glowing skin
Mahi-mahi	Protein, iron	Lean protein for strong muscles; healthy skin
Salmon	Omega-3s, monounsaturated ("good") fats	Improves circulation; shiny hair and bright skin; boosts brain health
Shrimp	Protein; vitamin B_{12}; selenium; iron	May help prevent Alzheimer's; improves mood; helps prevent high blood pressure
Tofu	Protein; iron; antioxidants; omega-3s; calcium	Strong bones and muscles; brain booster; aids with menopausal health

FWB	KEY NUTRIENTS	BENEFITS
Lean Protein—*Continued*		
Tuna	Protein, vitamin A, omega-3s	Boosts brain health; lowers blood pressure and cholesterol; healthy skin
Marvelous Mushrooms		
Cremini	Thiamin, riboflavin, niacin, vitamin B_6, selenium, zinc	Boost immunity; may help prevent Alzheimer's; help lower cholesterol; energy booster
Shiitake	Vitamin C, iron, protein, fiber	Boost immunity; good for overall health; may help lower cholesterol
Totally Roots and Tubers		
Beets	Folate, manganese, potassium	Healthy heart; may help prevent cancer; healthy liver functions
Carrots	Beta-carotene; vitamins C and K	Healthy eyes; may help prevent cancer and heart disease; help regulate blood sugar
Potatoes	Thiamin; niacin; vitamins C, B_6, K; fiber; folate; calcium; iron	Maintain healthy heart; help regulate blood pressure; healthy brain
Sweet potatoes	Beta-carotene, vitamin C, fiber, iron	Gorgeous skin; boost immunity; great for blood circulation
Vibrant Veggies		
Artichokes	Fiber; calcium; iron; thiamin; riboflavin; niacin; vitamins C and B_6	May stabilize blood sugar; natural diuretic; help protect liver
Asparagus	Thiamin; niacin; vitamins A, C, K, and B_6; fiber; manganese	Heart health; natural diuretic; healthy kidneys and lungs; bright eyes; may help prevent cancer
Bok choy	Calcium, potassium	Strong teeth and bones; helps with natural electrolyte balance
Cabbage	Vitamins B_6, C, and K; fiber; folate	Detoxifies body naturally; great for digestion; can help prevent breast cancer and Alzheimer's; overall cardio health

FWB	KEY NUTRIENTS	BENEFITS

Vibrant Veggies—*Continued*

FWB	KEY NUTRIENTS	BENEFITS
Eggplant	Thiamin, niacin, vitamin B_6, fiber, potassium	Brain booster; aids in cardio health; enhances immunity; natural diuretic
Garlic	Antioxidants, such as vitamins B_6 and C; manganese	Helps lower cholesterol and blood pressure; helps protect against infection; maintains normal blood sugar levels; keeps bones strong and healthy; antibacterial properties
Onions	Vitamin C, fiber	Antibacterial properties; strong bones; aid in digestion; may help prevent cancer
Pumpkin	Niacin; vitamins A, C, B_6, and B_5; potassium; fiber	Great for healthy lungs, beautiful eyes, supple skin
Red bell peppers	Vitamins A, C, K, and B_6; fiber	Healthy lungs; cardio health; bright eyes
Scallions	Thiamin; vitamins A and C; calcium	Help lower blood sugar and cholesterol; may help reduce risk of cancer; help with inflammation
Tomatoes	Lycopene; thiamin; riboflavin; niacin; vitamins A, B_6, C, and K; fiber; potassium	May help prevent cancer and protect your skin from wrinkles
Zucchini	Vitamins A and C; fiber; potassium; manganese	Natural anti-inflammatory properties; aid in digestion; help satiety

Whole Grains and Seeds

FWB	KEY NUTRIENTS	BENEFITS
Barley	Fiber, selenium, tryptophan	Boosts immunity; helps digestion; may help prevent cancer
Brown rice	Fiber; protein; manganese; antioxidants, such as selenium	Keeps you fuller longer and may aid in healthy weight management; lowers cholesterol; aids in digestion; may help prevent cancer
Flaxseeds	Omega-3s, monounsaturated ("good") fats, protein, fiber	Boost brain health; great for beautiful hair, nails, and skin; aid digestion
Oats	Fiber, protein, manganese, selenium	Help lower cholesterol and blood pressure; optimum kidney, liver, and spleen functions; protect against diabetes and heart disease

FWB	KEY NUTRIENTS	BENEFITS
Whole Grains and Seeds—*Continued*		
Quinoa	Protein, fiber, manganese, magnesium, iron, complete protein	Overall cardio health; aids in prevention of migraines; may help prevent cancer and heart disease; aids in digestion; lowers risk of type 2 diabetes
Soba noodles	Fiber, protein, iron	Help lower cholesterol; lower blood pressure; aid in digestion
Wheat bran	Fiber, protein, iron	Reduces risk of diabetes; aids digestion; may help prevent cancer
Whole wheat bread	Iron, protein, fiber	Keeps you fuller longer; good for digestion; may help prevent cancer

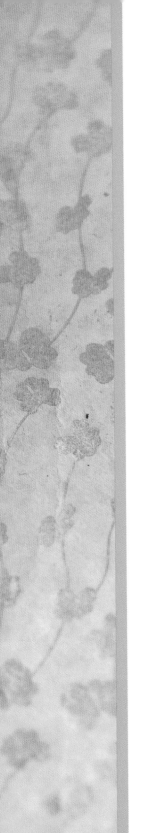

Ⓥ = vegetarian   🅥🅝 = vegan

CHAPTER 1

Brekkie & Brunch

Good morning, sunshine!

Morning is a critical time to fuel up with healthy and lean proteins, filling fiber, and antioxidants that will keep your glow on. If my schedule is super jam-packed, I'll start off with a pure energy booster like a 3-Veg Scramble (and take it to go in a low-cal whole wheat wrap if I don't have time to enjoy it at home). On lazy weekends I'll invite some girlfriends over for brunch (and gossip!) and cook up faves, like crêpes loaded with juicy peaches or seemingly sinful sticky buns. Of course we can have our cake (or crêpes!) and eat it, too—we just need to know how to get our skinny on. With some smart substitutions and swaps, you don't have to sacrifice pancakes or lemony scones for a skinny waistline.

If you think that oatmeal is for kids and grannys, then think again! This oatmeal recipe is anything but boring thanks to creamy nonfat yogurt and a few sweet berries. Oats are packed with protein, fiber, and iron, plus they're easy on the wallet. They're a seasonless pantry staple!
FWB: Oats

Berry Creamy Oatmeal

SERVES **4**

3 cups quick oats

1 cup nonfat plain Greek yogurt

$\frac{1}{4}$ cup honey

Pinch of ground cinnamon

Pinch of freshly grated nutmeg

Pinch of sea salt

$\frac{1}{2}$ pint blueberries, raspberries, or strawberries (about 1 cup)

4 teaspoons dark brown sugar (optional)

$\frac{1}{2}$ cup toasted sliced almonds (optional)

Bring 3 cups of water to a boil in a medium saucepan over high heat. Add the oats, stir, cover, and turn off the heat.

Once the oats are plump, about 4 minutes, stir in the yogurt, honey, cinnamon, nutmeg, and salt. Gently fold in the berries. If desired, sprinkle each serving with 1 teaspoon brown sugar and 2 tablespoons almonds. Now how easy was that?

Per serving: 366 calories, 5 g fat (0 g saturated, 0 g trans), 14 g protein, 8 g fiber, 25 g sugars, 120 mg sodium, 68 g carbohydrates, 0 mg cholesterol

♡ Frugal & Fab

Individually packed pouches of flavored quick oats are often high in sugar and contain more calories than you'd suspect. Be your smart self and DIY to save calories *and* change. Add in brown sugar, cinnamon, and raisins to taste.

These simple parfaits deliver everything I want in the morning: a speedy, healthy, sweet, low-fat, and antioxidant-packed start to the day. If you're more of a Greek yogurt goddess than a ricotta-mama, try it instead—it'll add a tangy tingle to your morning routine. FWB: Berries

Ricotta, Berry, and Runny Honey Parfaits

SERVES **4**

2 cups strawberries, halved

1 cup raspberries

1 cup blueberries or blackberries

1/2 cup part-skim ricotta cheese

Pourable honey, for serving

1/2 cup slivered almonds

Place the berries in a large colander and gently rinse under cold running water. Turn out onto a paper towel–lined baking sheet and shake the pan to dry the berries.

Divide the berries among 4 dessert bowls. Top with 2 tablespoons of ricotta, a drizzle of runny honey, and 2 tablespoons almonds. Then dig in and put those antioxidants to work!

Per serving: 189 calories, 9 g fat (1.5 g saturated, 0 g trans), 8 g protein, 6 g fiber, 16 g sugars, 77 mg sodium, 25 g carbohydrates, 10 mg cholesterol

Slim Scoop!

For a little extra zip, grate a pinch of lemon, lime, or orange zest over the berries before topping with the ricotta, nuts, and honey.

Whenever life hands me lemons, I make these lusciously lemony scones! They're best served with a sip of tea, great gossip, and your best friends—all the necessary ingredients to turn your day around in an instant. The Raspberry Cream Spread (page 9) is the perfect accessory. FWB: Dried cranberries

Lemon-Cran Scones

MAKES **12** SCONES

3 cups all-purpose flour plus extra for shaping

$\frac{1}{2}$ cup sugar

Grated zest and juice of 1 lemon

1 teaspoon baking powder

1 teaspoon baking soda

1 teaspoon salt

4 tablespoons unsalted butter, cut into $\frac{1}{2}$-inch cubes

$\frac{3}{4}$ cup low-fat buttermilk

$\frac{1}{4}$ cup unsweetened applesauce

1 cup dried cranberries

1 cup confectioners' sugar

Preheat the oven to 375°F. Line a baking sheet with parchment paper.

Whisk the flour, sugar, lemon zest, baking powder, baking soda, and salt together in a large bowl. Add the butter and work it in with your fingertips until there are no pieces larger than a small pea.

Whisk the buttermilk and applesauce together in a large liquid measuring cup. Add half of the buttermilk mixture to the flour mixture and stir with a fork. Pour in the remaining buttermilk mixture and add the dried cranberries. Stir until just combined.

Lightly flour a work surface. Divide the dough in half and sprinkle the top of each piece of dough with a little flour and then pat into a 1-inch-thick round that is about $5\frac{1}{4}$ inches in diameter. Using a long sharp knife or pizza wheel, divide each round into 6 wedges (like a pie). Place the wedges on the baking sheet and bake until golden, 15 to 18 minutes. Let cool for 5 minutes on the pan before transferring to a wire rack to cool completely.

While the scones cool, make the glaze. Whisk $\frac{1}{4}$ cup of lemon juice and the confectioners' sugar together in a small bowl. Use a spoon to drizzle the glaze over the cooled scones. Hold your horses for at least 5 minutes (to let the glaze set up) before serving.

Per scone: 259 calories, 4 g fat (3 g saturated, 0 g trans), 4 g protein, 1 g fiber, 26 g sugars, 349 mg sodium, 52 g carbohydrates, 11 mg cholesterol

Back in my surf-bum days in Hermosa Beach, I finished off most mornings at the best little café on LA's west side and always ate the same thing—a raspberry-oat muffin and a big cup of joe. I don't usually try to knock off recipes, but I had to try to re-create these muffins (with a healthy applesauce twist), if only to relive my carefree days of surf, sand, and SoCal fun. FWB: Oats, berries

Raspberry-Oat Muffins

MAKES **12** MUFFINS

$1^1/_2$ cups all-purpose flour

1 cup quick oats

$^3/_4$ cup packed light brown sugar

2 teaspoons ground cinnamon

1 teaspoon baking powder

$^1/_2$ teaspoon baking soda

Pinch of sea salt

2 large eggs

$^3/_4$ cup unsweetened applesauce

2 tablespoons honey

1 cup frozen raspberries

Confectioners' sugar

Raspberry Cream Spread
   (page 9)

♡ Frugal & Fab

Frozen berries are tons cheaper than out-of-season fresh berries! Plus they're picked at their peak deliciousness, so they often taste a whole lot better, too.

Preheat the oven to 400°F. Line a 12-cup muffin tin with paper liners.

Whisk the flour, oats, brown sugar, cinnamon, baking powder, baking soda, and salt together in a large bowl. Whisk the eggs, applesauce, and honey together in a medium bowl. Stir the applesauce mixture into the flour mixture until completely incorporated. Gently fold in the frozen raspberries.

Using a $1^1/_2$-ounce ice cream scoop, portion the batter into the paper cups, filling each about three-fourths full. Bake, rotating midway through cooking, until golden brown, the center of a muffin resists light pressure, and a toothpick inserted into the center of a muffin comes out clean, about 20 minutes.

Let cool for 20 minutes in the pan, then transfer to a wire rack to cool completely. Dust with confectioners' sugar and serve with the Raspberry Cream Spread.

Per muffin (without Raspberry Cream Spread): 180 calories, 1.5 g fat (0 g saturated, 0 g trans), 4 g protein, 2 g fiber, 20 g sugars, 122 mg sodium, 38 g carbohydrates, 35 mg cholesterol

So you're thinking, bran? Not so sexy. Well I beg to differ! Bran keeps you healthy, and feeling great is the most important ingredient for being the sexiest one on the block. Another cool bonus is that this batter can be made the night before, so in the morning all you have to do is scoop it into the pan and bake for a hot-from-the-oven treat. FWB: Wheat bran

Bright-Eye Blueberry-Bran Muffins

MAKES **12** MUFFINS

1½ cups wheat bran
1 cup all-purpose flour
1 teaspoon baking powder
½ teaspoon baking soda
Pinch of sea salt
1 large egg
½ cup packed light brown sugar
2 teaspoons honey
1 teaspoon vanilla extract
½ cup low-fat buttermilk
½ cup unsweetened applesauce
1 cup frozen blueberries
Confectioners' sugar, for dusting
Sweet Honey Spread (opposite page) or Apple Butter (page 24), optional

Preheat the oven to 375°F. Line a 12-cup muffin pan with paper liners.

Whisk the wheat bran, flour, baking powder, baking soda, and salt together in a medium bowl. Whisk the egg, brown sugar, honey, and vanilla together in a large bowl, then whisk in the buttermilk and applesauce. Stir in the flour mixture in three additions, mixing just until a few dry spots remain before adding more. Gently stir in the blueberries and mix just to incorporate (take care not to overmix so your batter doesn't toughen up and turn blue!).

Using a 1½-ounce ice cream scoop, portion the batter into the paper cups, filling each about three-fourths full. Bake, rotating midway through cooking, until golden on top, the center of a muffin resists light pressure, and a toothpick inserted into the center of a muffin comes out clean, about 20 minutes. Let cool for 20 minutes in the pan, then transfer to a wire rack to cool completely. Dust with confectioners' sugar.

Per muffin: 112 calories, 1 g fat (0 g saturated, 0 g trans), 14 g protein, 4 g fiber, 13 g sugars, 126 mg sodium, 26 g carbohydrates, 18 mg cholesterol

Slim Scoop!
Sometimes I'll bake a batch of muffins in a mini muffin tin and freeze them. Just 15 seconds in the microwave for a delicious solution to a sweets craving.

5 Skinny Spreads to Live By

Bagel with a schmear may be a quick breakfast fix, but it's not the smart way to start your day. I save a ton of calories and fat grams by making my own quick and easy skinny spreads. They're creamy and dreamy and will change your perception of "diet" food completely! Try these on English muffins or toast. And don't reserve them for breakfast; they're great with crudités or baked tortilla chips, or in wrap sandwiches.

Creamy Salsa Spread

½ cup part-skim ricotta cheese & 2 tablespoons salsa & 2 tablespoons chopped roasted red peppers

Sweet Honey Spread

½ cup part-skim ricotta cheese & ¼ cup nonfat plain Greek yogurt & 1 tablespoon honey & ½ teaspoon ground cinnamon

Totally TDF Guacamole Spread

1 ripe Hass avocado mashed with ½ cup nonfat Greek yogurt & 1 squeeze lemon or lime juice & 1 tablespoon salsa & salt and pepper to taste

2-Second Honey-Mustard

½ cup Dijon mustard & 1 tablespoon honey

Raspberry Cream Spread

½ cup part-skim ricotta cheese & ¼ cup nonfat plain Greek yogurt & 1 tablespoon raspberry all-fruit spread & 1 tablespoon honey

Toasted-Almond Sticky Buns

MAKES **12** STICKY BUNS

1½ cups sliced almonds

1 package active dry yeast

1 teaspoon sugar

¼ cup warm water

1 cup unsweetened almond milk, at room temperature

3 tablespoons plus ¼ cup honey

½ teaspoon sea salt

3¼ cups all-purpose flour, sifted, plus extra for kneading

1½ tablespoons unsalted butter, at room temperature

½ cup packed light brown sugar

1 teaspoon ground cinnamon

1 teaspoon freshly grated nutmeg

Preheat the oven to 350°F. Place 1 cup of the almonds on a rimmed baking sheet and place them in the oven until golden brown, 4 to 6 minutes. Transfer the almonds to a large plate and set aside to cool.

Whisk the yeast, sugar, and water together in a small bowl. Cover the bowl with plastic wrap and set aside for 5 minutes.

Whisk the almond milk, 3 tablespoons of the honey, and the salt together in a large bowl. Add 1 cup of the flour and whisk until smooth. Pour in the yeast mixture, then stir in the remaining 2¼ cups flour, mixing with a wooden spoon. Once the dough gets too difficult to mix with the spoon, use your hands to gently knead it until it comes together to make a ball.

Transfer the dough to a floured work surface and continue to knead it until the dough is completely smooth, about 6 minutes. Grease a large, clean bowl with ½ tablespoon of the butter. Place the dough ball in the bowl, turn over to coat in butter, and cover the bowl with a warm, damp towel (I like to wet a kitchen towel, wring it out, and microwave it for 45 seconds). Let the dough rise in a warm, draft-free spot until it has doubled, about 40 minutes.

(continued)

Coat a 10-inch round cake pan with cooking spray and set aside. Turn the dough out onto a floured work surface and roll it into a 12 × 13-inch rectangle about ¼ inch thick. Mix the toasted almonds, ¼ cup of the brown sugar, the cinnamon, and nutmeg together in a small bowl. Melt the remaining 1 tablespoon butter on the stovetop or in the microwave. Brush the dough with the melted butter and sprinkle evenly with a thin layer of the almond-spice mixture.

Cut the dough lengthwise into twelve 1-inch-wide strips. Roll the strips up, forming a tight roll. Place the buns spiral side up in the cake pan. Cover with a warm, damp towel and set aside until they've increased in size slightly, about 20 minutes.

Spread the tops of the buns with the remaining ¼ cup honey, ¼ cup brown sugar, and ½ cup almonds. Bake until golden brown, 20 to 25 minutes. Let cool in the pan for 5 minutes. Serve warm.

Per serving: 282 calories, 8 g fat (1.5 g saturated, 0 g trans), 6 g protein, 3 g fiber, 20 g sugars, 100 mg sodium, 48 g carbohydrates, 4 mg cholesterol

Slim Scoop!

Even my mom questioned my logic on this one—why not just roll the entire piece of dough into a log and then slice crosswise into pieces instead of slicing and rolling individually? I tried it both ways and because the dough is so lean, the buns are just prettier made this way. For me, these hot numbers are as much about the "wow!" factor as they are about taste!

Tofu is a healthy alternative to meats, cheese, and eggs and I try to work it into recipes whenever I can. In this one, I use extra-firm tofu instead of eggs for a good-on-the-lips and friendly-to-the-hips scramble. Sun-dried tomatoes add tons of flavor in addition to a good dose of the phytonutrient lycopene, an antioxidant and potential cancer fighter. FWB: Tofu

Tofu Scramble with Fresh Basil and Sun-Dried Tomatoes   SERVES 4

4 ounces unsalted dry-packed sun-dried tomatoes (about ¾ cup)

1 teaspoon garlic powder

1 teaspoon smoked paprika

1 teaspoon dried mixed herbs (like a French or Italian blend)

1 package (14 ounces) extra-firm tofu

1 tablespoon extra-virgin olive oil

1 small red onion, finely chopped

8 button or cremini mushroom caps, finely chopped

½ teaspoon sea salt

¼ cup fresh basil leaves, stacked, rolled, and thinly sliced crosswise into ribbons

Place the sun-dried tomatoes in a small bowl. Cover with hot water and set aside until they're plump and soft, about 20 minutes. Drain, then slice the tomatoes into thin strips and set aside.

Whisk the garlic powder, paprika, and mixed herbs together in a medium bowl. Crumble the tofu into the bowl and stir to coat with spices. Set the tofu aside for 15 minutes.

While the tofu absorbs the flavors, heat the olive oil in a large nonstick skillet over medium-high heat. Add the onion, mushrooms, and salt and cook, stirring often, until the onions are translucent and soft, about 4 minutes. Reduce the heat to medium, add the tofu and sun-dried tomatoes, and cook, stirring often, until the tofu is heated through, about 4 minutes. Sprinkle with the basil before serving.

Per serving: 223 calories, 10 g fat (1 g saturated, 0 g trans), 15 g protein, 5 g fiber, 13 g sugars, 841 mg sodium, 22 g carbohydrates, 0 mg cholesterol

Slim Scoop!

I'm big into FWBs that contain lycopene, like sun-dried tomatoes. Other sources include red-pigmented fruit such as carrots and watermelon, pink grapefruit, and fresh tomatoes.

Getting a healthy start when I know I'm facing a crazy day helps me stay balanced. Made with egg whites and a few spoonfuls of salsa stirred into the eggs, this scramble makes me feel great inside and out. Add some chopped lean deli ham or turkey to the egg mixture for extra oomph. Remember to save the yolks for the hair masks on page 247—reuse, recycle, girlfriend! FWB: Red bell peppers, beans, spinach

Skinny 3-Veg Scramble

SERVES **4**

6 large eggs

6 large egg whites

½ cup bottled salsa

Salt and ground black pepper

1 cup roasted red peppers, drained and chopped

1 cup spinach, coarsely chopped

1 cup canned black beans, rinsed and drained

1 cup finely chopped zucchini

1 teaspoon ground cumin

Toasted English muffin halves, whole wheat bread, or tomato slices for serving

Whisk the whole eggs, egg whites, salsa, 1 teaspoon salt, and 1 teaspoon black pepper together in a medium bowl. Add the roasted peppers, spinach, and beans and stir to combine. Set aside.

Heat a medium nonstick skillet over medium heat. Lightly coat with cooking spray. Add the zucchini and cumin and cook, stirring often, until softened, about 2 minutes. Pour in the egg mixture and using a heatproof rubber spatula, gently fold and stir the mixture until the eggs are set and cooked to your liking. Taste and season with more salt and black pepper if needed. Serve over English muffins, bread, or tomato slices.

Per serving (without bread or tomato): 218 calories, 8 g fat (2 g saturated, 0 g trans), 20 g protein, 5 g fiber, 5 g sugars, 1,407 mg sodium, 18 g carbohydrates, 317 mg cholesterol

♥ Frugal & Fab

When times are tight, here are three words to live by: Eggs are cheap! For brekkie, brunch, lunch, or dinner, eggs deliver protein and omegas (if you buy the omega-enriched type) and lots of other good stuff for very little green.

English Muffin Bar—
The Skinny Bagel Alternative!

This is one of the simplest (and skinniest) ways to have friends over for brunch without breaking the bank or your diet. English muffins have a lot less calories and carbs than bagels but still satisfy that morning starch craving. Add a few toppings and a breakfast cocktail and you have a totally delicious morning spread that makes everyone happy—from your über-health-conscious friends to your workout-addicted roomie!

Set the spread up from left to right. Place a toaster, forks and knives, and a platter of halved English muffins on the left side and all of the fixin's to the right. End the spread with an assortment of fresh and dried fruits and pitchers of Dirty Marys (page 19) or add a mimosa bar (page 21) as a fab entryway bev station!

Spreads

♥ Any of the 5 Skinny Spreads on page 9

♥ Light cream cheese

♥ Part-skim ricotta cheese

♥ Jams + marmalades (place a demitasse spoon alongside the jam so people remember to watch their spoonfuls!)

Proteins

♥ Pan-seared julienned deli ham or turkey

♥ Egg white scramble, either plain or gussied up

♥ Canned salmon flaked with a fork

Veggie toppings

♥ Sliced avocados

♥ Sliced tomatoes

♥ Roasted red peppers

♥ Steamed spinach

♥ Sautéed onions and mushrooms

Seasonings

♥ Capers

♥ Chopped chives

♥ Coarse salt and black pepper

♥ Chopped fresh basil

♥ Furikake (Japanese sesame and seaweed condiment)

♥ Grated Parmesan cheese

♥ Smoked paprika

Inspired by one of my favorite kids' books, this is a great way to get veggies onto our breakfast plates, especially the plates of kids. My Seuss-inspired recipe mixes a few egg whites in with the whole eggs to lighten up the calorie count, has some lean ham, and includes some zucchini for a double dose of green. Sam I am would definitely approve. FWB: Spinach, tomatoes

Green with Envy Eggs and Ham

SERVES 6

1 small zucchini

2 teaspoons extra-virgin olive oil

10 large egg whites

6 large eggs

2 cups baby spinach, rinsed, patted dry, and coarsely chopped

10 thin slices lean deli ham, cut into thin strips

12 large basil leaves, stacked, rolled, and thinly sliced crosswise into ribbons

1/4 cup grated Parmesan cheese

Large pinch of garlic powder

Ground white pepper and sea salt

2 large tomatoes, each sliced into 3 rounds

Cayenne

Use a vegetable peeler to shave the zucchini into long ribbons. Heat 1 teaspoon of the oil in a large nonstick skillet over medium heat. Add the zucchini and cook, stirring occasionally, until tender, 1 to 2 minutes. Transfer to a bowl.

Whisk the egg whites and whole eggs in a large bowl until combined. Stir in the spinach, ham, three-fourths of the basil, the Parmesan, garlic powder, 1/2 teaspoon pepper, and 1/4 teaspoon salt.

Heat the remaining 1 teaspoon oil in the same skillet over medium heat. Add the egg mixture and use a rubber spatula to stir the eggs gently so you get a big, fluffy scramble.

Heat the broiler. Arrange the tomato slices on a baking sheet, sprinkle with salt and pepper to taste, and broil until browned, 1 to 2 minutes.

Place a tomato slice on each plate and sprinkle with a pinch of cayenne. Top with the egg scramble and finish with a few zucchini ribbons. Serve sprinkled with the remaining basil.

Per serving: 162 calories, 8 g fat (2.5 g saturated, 0 g trans), 17 g protein, 1 g fiber, 3 g sugars, 510 mg sodium, 5 g carbohydrates, 219 mg cholesterol

A few small switcheroos make a big difference when it comes to whittling your waistline. Instead of a heavy hollandaise, these poached eggs get sauced with a combo of nonfat Greek yogurt, some low-fat mayo, and a little Dijon mustard. I top my bennys with smoked salmon (a splurge, but so worth it!) and avocados—they give me lots of richness in a naturally good way. FWB: Eggs

Skinny Eggs Benny

SERVES 4

Sauce

1/2 cup nonfat plain Greek yogurt

1/4 cup light mayonnaise

2 tablespoons Dijon mustard

2 tablespoons honey

1 tablespoon fresh lemon juice

Benny

1 Hass avocado, thinly sliced

1/2 lemon

Flaked sea salt

6 ounces sliced smoked salmon (about 8 pieces)

Rinsed capers, chopped chives, and smoked paprika for serving (optional)

4 large eggs

2 English muffins, halved

To make the sauce: Whisk together the yogurt, mayonnaise, mustard, and honey in a small saucepan. Warm the sauce over medium heat, stirring often, about 2 minutes, then keep warm over low heat, stirring occasionally.

To make the benny: Arrange the avocado on a platter and squeeze with a little lemon juice to keep it from browning. Sprinkle with a few pinches of flaked sea salt. Add the salmon to the platter, cover with plastic wrap, and set aside. If using, place the capers, chives, and paprika in a few small bowls or ramekins and set aside.

Fill a large saucepan with enough water to come halfway up the sides and bring to a boil, then reduce to a gentle simmer. Crack an egg in a small cup or ramekin and gently slide the egg into the simmering water. Repeat with the remaining eggs. Cook until the whites are set and the yolks are covered with a thin film, about 4 minutes. While the eggs poach, toast the English muffins and then place each half, cut-side up, on a plate.

Use a slotted spoon to transfer the poached eggs to the toasted English muffins. Top with some sauce and serve with the platter of avocados, salmon, and other toppings (if desired), letting your friends create their own benny plate.

Per serving: 441 calories, 21 g fat (4 g saturated, 0 g trans), 38 g protein, 3 g fiber, 11 g sugars, 421 mg sodium, 28 g carbohydrates, 519 mg cholesterol

Who says you can't live the fab life on a budget? The key to my delish Bloody Marys is to add a splash of juice from a jar of olives, so don't ever throw out that liquid gold again! (If you don't have enough olive juice, visit a market where they hand-pack olives and ask for a container with just olive brine.) This recipe makes enough for four cocktails; I like to make it in a pitcher.

Dirty Marys

MAKES **6** COCKTAILS

2 cups low-sodium tomato juice

1 cup vodka (you don't need the super premium stuff)

1 cup olive juice

1 tablespoon prepared horseradish

A few good shakes of Worcestershire sauce

A few good shakes of hot sauce

1 lime, cut into wedges

6 celery stalks

Whisk the tomato juice, vodka, olive juice, horseradish, Worcestershire, and hot sauce together in a large pitcher. Fill 6 glasses with ice, pour the juice over the ice, add a squeeze of lime and serve with a celery stalk stirrer.

Note: Keep it classy in the drinks department. It's definitely not sexy to overdo it—all things in moderation.

Per cocktail: 149 calories, 4 g fat (0 g saturated, 0 g trans), 1 g protein, 1 g fiber, 3 g sugars, 720 mg sodium, 5 g carbohydrates, 0 mg cholesterol

It wouldn't be brunch without a flute of something bubbly, but remember that alcohol adds calories and subtracts from your bank account, so save it for celebrations and special occasions.

Candice's Can-Do Mimosas

MAKES 1 COCKTAIL

¼ cup sparkling wine

Pinch of grated fresh ginger

2 tablespoons orange, pineapple, or cranberry juice; mango nectar; or passion fruit puree

Fresh pomegranate seeds, fresh raspberries, for garnish

Pour the sparkling wine into a champagne flute. Add the ginger plus your choice of fruit juice. Garnish with fresh fruit as desired.

♥ Frugal & Fab

Think you can't afford sparkling wine? Think again! Since each glass of these mimosas mixes sparkling vino with juice, you're getting double your money's worth and stretching the alcohol for twice as many people. Instead of champagne, I make mine with less pricey sparkly like Cava (from Spain—also my grandfather's fave!), Italian Prosecco, or good ol' made-in-Cali sparkling wine (check out those from Mendocino, Carneros, and Sonoma). Since the sparkling wine is acting as a mixer with fruit juice, chances are your guests won't even detect the cash-saving swapout.

So easy, so fabulous, so dreamy, so classic! Stuffed with lusciously ripe peaches, these crêpes are rich, sweet, and decadent. At only 40 calories per cup, almond milk is a great lean substitute for regular milk that's really worth trying. FWB: Almond milk, yogurt

Peaches and Cream Crêpes

SERVES 4

$^1/_2$ cup plus 2 tablespoons unsweetened almond milk

1 large egg

1 cup all-purpose flour

$^1/_2$ teaspoon ground cinnamon

$^1/_2$ teaspoon freshly grated nutmeg

$^1/_4$ teaspoon sea salt

1 tablespoon plus 4 teaspoons honey

1 tablespoon unsalted butter, melted

$^1/_4$ cup chopped walnuts

2 teaspoons canola oil

2 peaches, peeled and thinly sliced

1 cup nonfat plain Greek yogurt

Preheat the oven to 350°F. Whisk the almond milk, egg, and $^1/_4$ cup water together in a medium bowl until well combined. Whisk together the flour, cinnamon, nutmeg, and salt in a separate bowl. Add the flour mixture to the almond milk mixture. Whisk a few times just to work the flour mixture in a bit, then add 1 tablespoon of the honey and the butter. Continue to whisk until the batter is smooth. (The batter can be made the night before and refrigerated until using.) Set the batter aside to rest while you toast the walnuts.

Place the walnuts in a small dry skillet. Toast them over medium heat until fragrant and lightly browned, 6 to 8 minutes, shaking the skillet often. Transfer to a large plate to cool.

Heat a medium nonstick skillet over medium heat. Add $^1/_4$ teaspoon of the oil to the skillet and swirl to coat (or lightly coat with cooking spray). Ladle about $^1/_4$ cup of batter into the skillet. Using the back of the ladle and working in a circular motion, spread the batter into an even, paper-thin layer, or tilt and swirl the skillet to evenly distribute the batter. Cook the crêpe until dry around the edges and golden-brown, about 1 minute, then use a heatproof rubber spatula to lift and flip the crêpe. Cook the second side until golden-brown, about 30 seconds. Transfer the crêpe to a large plate. Repeat with the remaining batter and oil (or cooking spray).

Place a crêpe on a large plate or a cutting board. Arrange a few peach slices in the center of the crêpe. Top with 2 tablespoons of yogurt, sprinkle with ½ tablespoon toasted walnuts, and finish with a ½ teaspoon of honey. Fold the crêpe in half, then in half again to make a wedge shape. Repeat with the remaining crêpes, serving 2 crêpes per person.

Per serving: 311 calories, 10 g fat (3 g saturated, 0 g trans), 12 g protein, 3 g fiber, 19 g sugars, 189 mg sodium, 45 g carbohydrates, 61 mg cholesterol

♥ Frugal & Fab

Using in-season fruit is usually the cheapest way to go. If there are no peaches around, try fresh strawberries, mango slices, or a buttery-ripe Bartlett pear. Frozen and canned fruit (packed in unsweetened juice) is a great cheapie sub-in, too; just remember to check the label to be sure there's no added sugar.

These pancakes capture the essence of fall. The pumpkin puree and applesauce work together to create tons of moisture and richness. All you need to make my seriously easy apple butter is three ingredients and a little time. The result is an über-sweet and delectable spread that's fantastic on these pancakes or on cinnamon toast with a dollop of nonfat Greek yogurt. FWB: Pumpkin

Pumpkin Pie Pancakes with Apple Butter

SERVES **6**

Apple Butter

1 jar (24 ounces) unsweetened applesauce

½ cup granulated sugar

1 tablespoon pumpkin pie spice

Pancakes

2 cups all-purpose flour

6 tablespoons light brown sugar

2 teaspoons baking powder

2 teaspoons pumpkin pie spice

½ teaspoon sea salt

¾ cup unsweetened pumpkin puree

⅔ cup unsweetened almond milk

4 large eggs

½ cup unsweetened applesauce

Confectioners' sugar (optional)

Use a turkey baster to transfer pancake batter neatly from bowl to skillet. Sounds silly ('cause it is!), but it totally works.

To make the apple butter: Whisk the applesauce, granulated sugar, and pumpkin pie spice together in a medium saucepan over medium-low heat. Cook, stirring every 20 minutes, until reduced to 1 cup, about 1½ hours. Let cool to room temperature.

To make the pancakes: Preheat the oven to 350°F. Whisk the flour, brown sugar, baking powder, pumpkin pie spice, and salt together in a large bowl. Whisk the pumpkin puree, almond milk, eggs, and applesauce together in a medium bowl. Add to the flour mixture using a rubber spatula to stir gently until just combined. The batter will be thick.

Heat a large nonstick skillet over medium heat. Coat the pan with cooking spray. Make 3 pancakes using ⅓ cup of batter for each. Cook until the outer edges firm up and the bottom is golden-brown, about 1½ minutes. Flip and cook the other side until golden brown, about another 1½ minutes. Transfer the pancakes to a rimmed baking sheet and set aside. Continue making pancakes, moving them to the baking sheet as they're cooked. Pop the baking sheet in the oven and cook the pancakes for an additional 5 minutes. Serve with a dusting of confectioners' sugar (if desired) and a schmear of apple butter.

Per serving: 392 calories, 4 g fat (1 g saturated, 0 g trans), 9 g protein, 4 g fiber, 44 g sugars, 370 mg sodium, 81 g carbohydrates, 141 mg cholesterol

Browned slices of lean deli ham satisfy my bacon cravings and give me a hammy hit without all of the calories and fat. I save even more calories and fat by adding a little maple syrup to some ricotta for a maple spread instead of adding a pat of butter and pool of syrup to every waffle. Last but certainly not least, I leave the apple peels on the apples for a healthy fiber boost. You've just got to love that fiber, honey! FWB: Whole wheat flour

Country Girl Waffle Stacks

MAKES **8** SQUARE WAFFLES

2 Granny Smith apples, halved and thinly sliced

1 teaspoon ground cinnamon

$^1/_2$ teaspoon freshly grated nutmeg

4 tablespoons maple syrup

1 cup part-skim ricotta cheese

2 cups whole wheat flour

3 tablespoons light brown sugar

2 teaspoons baking soda

$^1/_2$ teaspoon salt

1$^3/_4$ cups low-fat buttermilk

2 large eggs

1$^1/_2$ teaspoons canola oil

8 slices lean, low-sodium deli ham or turkey

Preheat the oven to 250°F. Place a rimmed baking sheet in the oven. Place the apples in a medium bowl and toss with the cinnamon, nutmeg, and 2 tablespoons of the maple syrup and set aside. Stir the ricotta and remaining 2 tablespoons maple syrup together in a small bowl and set aside.

Whisk the flour, brown sugar, baking soda, and salt together in a large bowl. Whisk the buttermilk and eggs together until combined in a small bowl. Add the buttermilk mixture to the flour mixture and stir to combine.

Heat a waffle iron according to the manufacturer's instructions. Coat the iron with cooking spray. Add enough batter to fill the holes without overflowing once the iron is closed. Cook until gorgeous and browned. Remove the waffle from the iron and place it on the baking sheet in the oven to stay warm while you cook the rest.

While you cook the waffles, heat a large nonstick skillet over medium-high heat. Add $^1/_2$ teaspoon of the oil to the skillet (or coat with cooking spray). Place a few slices of ham in the pan (the ham should lie flat in the skillet) and cook on both sides until lightly browned, 1$^1/_2$ to 2 minutes total. Transfer to a plate

(*continued*)

and repeat with the remaining ham, adding cooking spray if needed. Once all of the ham is browned, wipe out the skillet, heat over medium heat, and add the remaining 1 teaspoon oil (or coat with cooking spray). Add the apples, cooking them over medium heat until they're warm, 2 to 3 minutes.

Once all of the waffles are cooked, spread each with about 2 tablespoons of the maple-ricotta spread. Top with 1 slice of ham, cover with a few apple slices and serve.

Per waffle: 276 calories, 5 g fat (2 g saturated, 0 g trans), 15 g protein, 5 g fiber, 20 g sugars, 720 mg sodium, 46 g carbohydrates, 71 mg cholesterol

Slim Scoop!

Wrap leftover waffles in individual plastic wrap packages and store in a gallon-size resealable freezer bag. Re-warmed in a toaster, homemade frozen waffles make a great morning brekkie fix. Grab them along with your makeup bag, car keys, two cell phones, and a few magazines . . . oh wait, that's just my insane life! Nevertheless, waffles to go are the way to go!

El Ultimo Brekkie Burrito Bar

If I had to pick one last meal on this Earth, it would definitely be a California-style breakfast burrito loaded with fresh avocados and salsa galore—yum! In fact, I don't know many people who don't love breakfast burritos, which is why the brekkie burrito bar has become one of my all-time favorite brunch buffets. It's really easy to put together and, best yet, your friends get to customize their own burritos so it's all *bueno*. Here's a list of my faves for el ultimo burrito fiesta! Pick and choose what you want to serve, or do it up *grande*-style.

The setup: At the far left side of the table, stack a bunch of plates (one for each person) and a stack of warmed 10-inch whole wheat tortillas (you can keep them warm in a specially designed tortilla warmer or by wrapping them in warm kitchen towels). Serve your proteins of choice directly from the skillets they are made in to keep them warm, and set each on a trivet. Arrange bowls of veggies and seasonings, and place the sprinkles in small ramekins—perfect for pinches. Make sure you have lots of serving spoons—at least one for each bowl—and plenty of napkins!

Proteins

- Tofu Scramble (page 13)
- Skinny 3-Veg Scramble (page 14)
- Pan-seared chicken sausage, finely chopped
- Thick-sliced lean deli ham, chopped into cubes and pan-seared

Veggies

- Sautéed mushrooms, onions, and/or bell peppers
- Chopped tomatoes
- Canned black beans, rinsed
- Chopped bell peppers
- Baby spinach
- Sliced avocados

Seasonings

- Store-bought salsa or Black Bean Salsa (page 148)
- Nonfat Greek yogurt (skip the sour cream!)
- SoCali Guacamole (page 35)
- Chopped roasted red peppers
- Canned sweet corn, drained
- Hot sauce—a SoCal must!

Sprinkles

- Ground cumin
- Dried oregano
- Red-pepper flakes
- Chopped cilantro
- Crumbled cheese like Mexican Cotija

Ⓥ = vegetarian Ⓥⓝ = vegan

CHAPTER 2

Minis & Munchies

Mini bites, dips, and munchies are "in" in a big way, and I especially love this kind of food for socializing. I've given many of these classic party starters a total facelift so they're supertasty and even good for you. Some of my most requested recipes are in this chapter, like spinach-artichoke dip that has loads less fat than your old standby, and my super juicy sliders (you'd never guess that they're made from lean beef). By the way, you should know that these recipes will save you more than just calories—for the price of a couple of cans of chickpeas and some raw veggies for dipping, you can serve up a big bowl of TDF Hummus (page 49) to keep everyone full, fit, and happy. Mini munchies like BLTs and sliders also deliver a perfect three-bite eat while keeping costs minimized.

Skinny Mini BLT Bites

MAKES **6** MINI SANDWICHES

4 large or 6 medium slices whole wheat bread

2 teaspoons extra-virgin olive oil

Sea salt

Garlic powder

4 slices lean turkey bacon

1 Hass avocado, halved, pitted, and peeled

2 tablespoons 2-Second Honey-Mustard (page 9)

2 small plum tomatoes, cut crosswise into six $\frac{1}{4}$-inch-thick rounds

12 baby lettuce leaves

$\frac{1}{2}$ lemon or lime

Slim Scoop!

Save calories without sacrificing! Buy thinly sliced loaves of whole wheat bread versus thicker cut slices. I also find that sprinkling deli meat with a little smoked paprika adds a nice smoky flavor for no added calories.

Preheat the oven to 350°F. Using a 2-inch round or heart-shaped cookie cutter, punch out 2 to 3 circles from each slice of bread for 12 circles in all. Using a pastry brush, dab one side of each round of bread with a little olive oil. Season with a pinch of salt and some garlic powder and place seasoned-side up on a baking sheet and set aside.

Cut the turkey bacon crosswise into 2-inch lengths. Place the bacon on a second baking sheet. Place both baking sheets in the oven and bake until the bread is golden brown and toasted, and the bacon is crisp and browned, 15 to 20 minutes.

Slice each avocado half crosswise, then cut lengthwise into $\frac{1}{4}$-inch-wide slices. Sprinkle with a little lemon or lime juice to prevent browning and set aside.

Assemble the sandwiches: Spread 1 teaspoon of the honey-mustard on the seasoned side of half of the toast circles. Top with 2 pieces of bacon, a tomato slice, 2 lettuce leaves, and a couple of avocado slices. Top with a second toast circle, seasoned-side down.

Per sandwich: 153 calories, 7 g fat (1 g saturated, 0 g trans), 7 g protein, 4 g fiber, 3 g sugars, 321 mg sodium, 17 g carbohydrates, 13 mg cholesterol

While pulling together some guac for girls' night in, I discovered that I was short on avocados. Since the amount I had couldn't possibly feed the number of hungry gals on their way, I reached for the nonfat Greek yogurt. The yogurt bulked up the quantity without any fat and added a nice tang to boot. Paired with lean and tasty homemade chips, I had accidentally stumbled on a win-win combo. FWB: Avocado, nonfat yogurt

SoCali Guacamole and Home-Baked Chips

SERVES **8**

Chips

1 teaspoon dried oregano

1/4 teaspoon cayenne

1/2 teaspoon sea salt

8 flour or whole wheat tortillas

4 teaspoons extra-virgin olive oil

Guacamole

3 Hass avocados

1/2 small yellow onion, finely chopped

1/4 cup nonfat plain Greek yogurt

1 tablespoon soy sauce

1/8 teaspoon cayenne

1/4 teaspoon sea salt

1/2 lime

Slim Scoop!

For an even skinnier version, serve the guac with jicama sticks doused with fresh lime juice and a sprinkle of cayenne.

To make the chips: Preheat the oven to 350°F. Mix the oregano, cayenne, and salt together in a small bowl or ramekin. Brush each tortilla with a little of the olive oil. Sprinkle with the herb-spice mixture. Halve the tortillas and then cut each half into 4 wedges. Place the tortilla wedges on two rimmed baking sheets so they just barely touch one another (you may need to do this in two batches). Bake until browned and crisp, 12 to 14 minutes, rotating the baking sheet midway through cooking. Set aside to cool completely before transferring to a large serving bowl.

To make the guacamole: Halve and pit the avocados. Scoop out the flesh and place in a medium bowl. With a fork, gently smash and stir the avocado, breaking it up into a chunky mass. Add the onion and yogurt and stir to combine. Add the soy sauce, cayenne, salt, and a squeeze of lime juice. Stir to combine and taste with a chip, adding more salt if needed. Serve it up to your hungry crew, preferably straight away (or cover with plastic wrap and refrigerate for a few hours, tops).

Per serving: 348 calories, 15 g fat (3 g saturated, 0 g trans), 8 g protein, 6 g fiber, 1 g sugars, 565 mg sodium, 46 g carbohydrates, 0 mg cholesterol

Not only are these sliders to die for (TDF baby!), they might just possibly be the recipe of the century! Every time I teach friends the recipe they go nutzo because no one believes that something that tastes so good can actually be low in fat. But hey, that's the point, right? It's not diet food (boo on diet food!), it's to-die-for made healthy. FWB: Lean ground beef

TDF Sliders with Caramelized Onions and Mushrooms
MAKES **8** MINI BURGERS

1 tablespoon plus 2 teaspoons extra-virgin olive oil

1 cup finely chopped cremini mushroom caps (about 3 ounces)

1 small red onion, finely chopped

1 garlic clove, finely minced

$1/4$ cup finely chopped parsley

$1/2$ teaspoon dried oregano

$1/2$ teaspoon sea salt

1 pound 96% lean ground beef

8 King's Hawaiian sweet rolls or small, soft dinner rolls

2 plum tomatoes, thinly sliced

8 pickle slices (optional)

2-Second Honey-Mustard (page 9) or Skinny 'Cue Sauce (page 176) for serving

Heat 1 tablespoon of the oil in a medium nonstick skillet over medium heat. Add the mushrooms, onion, and garlic and cook, stirring often, until the onions are soft and golden brown, about 4 minutes. Stir in the parsley, oregano, and salt. Transfer the mixture to a medium bowl to cool.

Place the beef in a large bowl, add the cooled mushroom mixture, and gently fold the two together. Divide the beef mixture into 8 equal balls and then gently form each into a semi-compact $2^{1}/_{2}$- to 3-inch-thick patty. Split the rolls in half and brush the cut sides with some of the remaining 2 teaspoons olive oil. Set aside.

Heat a nonstick grill pan over medium-high heat for 2 minutes. Add the burgers and grill on each side until browned, about 2 minutes per side for medium. Transfer to a plate while you grill the rolls, cut-sides down, until golden and etched with grill marks from the pan, about 1 minute. Place each patty on a bun bottom and top with a slice of tomato, a pickle slice, if desired, and the bun top. Serve with the Honey-Mustard or 'Cue Sauce on the side.

Per burger: 200 calories, 5 g fat (0.5 g saturated, 0 g trans), 6 g protein, 2 g fiber, 11 g sugars, 661 mg sodium, 33 g carbohydrates, 5 mg cholesterol

Quick "Under 2 Hundy" Skinny Snacks

Besides clocking in at less than 200 calories, these grab-and-go eats are naturally delicious. Keep the ingredients handy to satisfy your sweet and salty cravings.

♥ 1 baguette slice & 1 tomato slice & 1 teaspoon grated Pecorino Romano cheese & 1 basil leaf

♥ 1 apple, sliced & 2 tablespoons TDF Hummus (page 49)

♥ 1 nectarine, chopped & 1 tablespoon toasted almonds & 1 teaspoon honey

♥ 1 small cucumber (halved and seeds scooped to make a "boat") & 2 tablespoons SoCali Guacamole (page 35) & 2 tablespoons chopped roasted red peppers

♥ 2 tablespoons raw almonds & 1 tablespoon dried cranberries & 1 tablespoon raisins

♥ 1 small banana & 1 tablespoon fat-free chocolate syrup & 1 tablespoon chopped walnuts

♥ 1 small cucumber (halved and seeds scooped to make a "boat") & 2 tablespoons TDF Hummus (page 49) & pinch of smoked paprika

♥ 1 celery stalk & 1 tablespoon almond butter & 1 tablespoon raisins

♥ 1 large hard-cooked egg & 1 teaspoon chopped chives & pinch of smoked paprika

♥ ¼ cup whole wheat pretzel sticks & 1 tablespoon dried cranberries & 1 tablespoon raw cashews

Two grilled cheese sandwiches make a great snack for four people. I absolutely love these grilled cheese fingers dunked in the tomato soup on page 84. For a fancy presentation, accessorize the fingers by wrapping a thin strip of parchment paper around the center and taping the two ends together (see photo page 85). FWB: Whole wheat bread

Totally Un-Croque Monsieur Fingers

SERVES **4**

1 tablespoon Dijon mustard

1 teaspoon light mayonnaise

4 slices whole wheat or whole grain bread

6 ultra-thin slices Asiago, Gruyère, or Cheddar cheese

6 slices lean deli chicken, ham, or turkey (optional)

2 teaspoons extra-virgin olive oil

Mix the mustard and mayonnaise together in a small bowl and spread 2 of the bread slices with the Dijonnaise. Top with 2 slices of cheese and 3 slices of deli meat, if desired, then cover with a final slice of cheese. Place the remaining bread slices on top.

Heat the olive oil in a medium nonstick skillet over medium heat. Add the sandwiches (you should hear them sizzle when they hit the pan) and grill until browned, about 2 minutes. Flip over and brown the other side, 1 to $1\frac{1}{2}$ minutes longer (check the second side often as it usually browns more quickly than the first).

Transfer the sandwiches to a cutting board and let them cool for 2 minutes before removing the crusts with a serrated knife and slicing each sandwich lengthwise into 4 even fingers. Serve hot.

Per serving: 154 calories, 8 g fat (3 g saturated, 0 g trans), 7 g protein, 2 g fiber, 2 g sugars, 369 mg sodium, 13 g carbohydrates, 13 mg cholesterol

Having grown up with a Japanese mother and a Polish-American father, pierogis and gyoza are two of my favorite snacks ever, with gyoza a standard in the Kumai-Gwiazdowski household. I call my mom's cooking technique "freaming," half frying and half steaming. It saves you calories and fat since you use half as much oil. If you prefer to sub ground pork for the ground beef, no problemo. FWB: Shiitake mushrooms

Mom's Homemade Gyoza

MAKES ABOUT **30** POTSTICKERS

Dipping sauce

¼ cup reduced-sodium soy sauce

¼ cup rice vinegar

Scallions, sliced on the diagonal

Gyoza

1 pound 96% lean ground beef

5 dried shiitake mushrooms soaked in boiling water 5 minutes, drained, and chopped

5 scallions, finely chopped

1 small yellow onion, finely chopped

3 large green cabbage leaves, finely chopped

4 garlic cloves, minced

¼ cup reduced-sodium soy sauce

2 tablespoons dark sesame oil

1 teaspoon grated fresh ginger

1 teaspoon sugar

All-purpose flour

30 round wonton skins (about ½ package)

6 teaspoons canola or vegetable oil

To make the sauce: Whisk the soy sauce and vinegar together in a small dish. Add the scallions and set aside.

To make the gyoza: Mix the ground beef, mushrooms, scallions, onion, cabbage, and garlic together in a large bowl. Whisk the soy sauce, sesame oil, ginger, and sugar together in a small bowl. Add the soy sauce mixture to the beef mixture and stir together until combined.

Sprinkle a work surface with some flour. Place a small bowl of warm water next to your work area. Place a wonton wrapper on the floured area and place 2 teaspoons of the beef mixture in the center. Dip a finger in the warm water and moisten the edges of the wrapper, then fold the wrapper over the filling (as if you were making a turnover) and press the edges together. Use your index finger and thumb to pinch the edges so they have a cute ruffled look (like the edge of a pie crust). Set aside and repeat with the rest of the filling and wrappers.

Heat 1½ teaspoons of canola oil in a large nonstick skillet over medium-high heat for 2 minutes. Add about 10 gyoza to the pan and cook until the bottoms are golden brown, 1 to 2 minutes (when peeking under the gyoza to check the color, be gentle— these little guys are fragile!). Add ¼ cup of water to the skillet, reduce the heat to medium, cover, and cook without turning

(continued)

Fresh ginger adds a ton of flavor to salad dressings and sauces. Instead of buying a big whole "hand" at the market, feel free to break off just what you need. A 1-inch piece yields about 1 tablespoon of minced ginger.

until the wrappers are translucent, about 2 minutes. Uncover and cook until the water has evaporated and the filling is cooked through, 2 to 3 minutes longer.

Remove the pan from the heat. Pour any liquid remaining in the pan into a bowl. Place a large plate over the skillet (the plate should be larger than the skillet) and flip the pan over—the gyoza should effortlessly fall from the pan to the plate revealing their gorgeous golden brown skins. Gyoza taste best when hot, so serve immediately with the dipping sauce as you cook up the next batch. Cook 2 more batches, adding a tiny bit more oil as needed and $\frac{1}{4}$ cup water for each batch. Wipe out the skillet between batches if necessary.

Per potsticker: 66 calories, 3 g fat (0.5 g saturated, 0 g trans), 4 g protein, 1 g fiber, 1 g sugars, 292 mg sodium, 6 g carbohydrates, 9 mg cholesterol

DIY Fresh Spring Roll Bar

A spring roll DIY bar is fabulous for parties and get-togethers—familiar yet a little exotic (kind of like me!). I've been known to use the pretty array of veggies—like bright peppers and green herbs—as a stand-in for flowers!

The setup: At the far left have a stack of small plates. Next, put out a dozen 8½-inch spring roll wrappers (available in Asian markets and the produce section of some supermarkets). Next to the wrappers, have a shallow bowl (as big in diameter as the wrappers) filled with warm water. Follow with the fillings and a variety of condiments in cute bowls. Then sit back and let your friends roll with it.

Proteins
- Seared Garlicky Shrimp or Tofu (page 46)

Vegetables
- Red bell peppers, cut into long, thin strips
- Shredded carrots
- Bean sprouts
- Sugar snap peas, blanched for 2 to 3 minutes in boiling water, shocked in ice water, and thinly sliced on the diagonal
- Snow peas, thinly sliced on the diagonal
- Sweet corn, preferably grilled or broiled (for a smoky flavor), kernels sliced off the cob

Seasonings
- Toasted sesame seeds
- Scallions, thinly sliced on the diagonal, or chopped chives
- Hot sauce (I like sriracha)
- Teriyaki sauce
- Whole basil leaves
- Whole cilantro leaves
- Chinese Chop peanut dressing (page 52)

How to wrap a spring roll: Dip the wrapper in the warm water for 10 seconds, then lay it on a plate. Place 1 tablespoon of shrimp or tofu filling in the bottom third of the wrapper and slightly spread out horizontally, but leaving a 1-inch border at the edges. Sprinkle with some vegetables (not too many now!) and seasonings of choice. Fold the sides over the filling and then fold the bottom up and over the filling, rolling the spring roll tightly. Place it seam-side down and cut in half diagonally. Serve the Chinese Chop dressing on the side.

Per spring roll (2 tablespoons vegetables, 1 heaping tablespoon garlicky shrimp, 1 teaspoon peanut dressing): 81 calories, 5 g fat (0.5 g saturated, 0 g trans), 5 g protein, 1 g fiber, 2 g sugars, 100 mg sodium, 6 g carbohydrates, 29 mg cholesterol

I often use 31/40 count peeled and cleaned shrimp, meaning there are 31 to 40 shrimp to a pound. Because they're bite-size, I save time by not having to chop them, and small shrimp are a bargain compared to the big guys! For a vegetarian version, sub one 14-ounce package of extra-firm tofu for the shrimp. FWB: Shiitake mushrooms

Seared Garlicky Shrimp Filling for Spring Rolls

MAKES ENOUGH FOR **12** 8½-INCH SPRING ROLLS

2 tablespoons canola or vegetable oil

1 small yellow onion, very finely chopped

15 fresh shiitake mushrooms (5 ounces), stems discarded, caps very finely chopped, or 7 dried shiitake mushrooms covered in boiling water 5 minutes, drained, and chopped

2 garlic cloves, minced

1 tablespoon grated fresh ginger

½ pound peeled and deveined small shrimp

1 teaspoon reduced-sodium soy sauce

Heat the oil in a large skillet or wok over medium-high heat. Add the onion and cook until starting to soften, 1 to 2 minutes. Add the mushrooms and cook, stirring often, until soft, about 3 minutes. Stir in the garlic and ginger and cook until the garlic is fragrant, about 1 minute, stirring often. Add the shrimp and soy sauce and cook until the shrimp curl and become opaque, 1 to 2 minutes, stirring often. Transfer to a medium serving bowl and set aside to cool. (Refrigerate if you're not using the filling within 30 minutes.)

Per serving: 50 calories, 2.7 g fat (0 g saturated, 0 g trans), 4 g protein, 0.5 g fiber, 0 g sugars, 45 mg sodium, 3 g carbohydrates, 28 mg cholesterol

Beautiful Black Bean and Banana Empanadas

MAKES **12** EMPANADAS

2 tablespoons extra-virgin olive oil

1 medium zucchini, finely chopped

1/2 yellow onion, finely chopped

1/2 red bell pepper, finely chopped

2 garlic cloves, minced

1 teaspoon ground cumin

1 teaspoon chili powder

1/4 teaspoon cayenne

1 teaspoon sea salt

1 can (15 ounces) black beans, rinsed and drained

3/4 cup mashed ripe banana (1 large or 2 medium)

All-purpose flour for rolling the dough

1 pound prepared pizza dough

1 teaspoon dried oregano

6 tablespoons nonfat plain Greek yogurt

3 tablespoons chopped cilantro

Adjust an oven rack to the lower middle position and preheat the oven to 400°F. Line a rimmed baking sheet with parchment paper.

Heat 1 tablespoon of the oil in a large nonstick skillet over medium heat. Add the zucchini, onion, bell pepper, and garlic and cook, stirring often, until they are very soft and browned, 5 to 7 minutes (if they brown too quickly, reduce the heat to medium-low). Stir in the cumin, chili powder, cayenne, and 1/2 teaspoon of the salt. Add the black beans, reduce the heat to medium-low, and cook until the beans are heated through and have absorbed some flavor, about 2 minutes. Add the mashed banana and cook, stirring often, until fragrant and thick, about 2 minutes. Set aside to cool completely.

Flour a cutting board. Divide the pizza dough in half and each half into 6 pieces (so you have 12 pieces total). Shape each piece into a ball and set aside to rest at least 10 minutes. Using a rolling pin, roll each dough ball into a 4-inch-diameter round about 1/4 inch thick.

Place about 2 tablespoons of the filling on the lower third of each round. Brush the bottom edge with some water and fold the top part over, pressing the edges together to seal. Press with

(continued)

the tines of a fork to make a decorative edge. Place the filled empanadas on the baking sheet.

Mix the oregano with the remaining $\frac{1}{2}$ teaspoon salt. Brush the tops of the empanadas with the remaining 1 tablespoon olive oil and then sprinkle with the oregano-salt blend. Bake until golden brown, about 30 minutes, rotating the pan midway through cooking. Transfer to a wire rack to cool slightly before serving with a dollop of yogurt and some chopped cilantro.

Per empanada: 149 calories, 4 g fat (0.5 g saturated, 0 g trans), 5 g protein, 3 g fiber, 4 g sugars, 359 mg sodium, 26 g carbohydrates, 0 mg cholesterol

Slim Scoop!

Don't skip this recipe just because you roll solo. Make, divide, and store for lunches or dinners. Or better yet, invite your crew over to share the wealth!

Slim Scoop!

Look at an ingredient list like a vitamin and mineral checklist and ask yourself what each ingredient is going to do for your body. I like to make sure that whatever I eat supplies me with the most fuel and nutritional benefits—what we get out of food is just as important as what we put into it to give it great flavor.

I slather hummus on just about everything! It makes a simple carrot stick taste like a million bucks and is a way healthier option than reaching for the cheese and crackers or chips. My to-die-for (TDF) hummus is a great dip for company, and leftovers are awesome on a skinny 'wich. Serve with some or all of the suggested dippers. FWB: Chickpeas

TDF Hummus with Veggie Sticks

SERVES 12

Hummus

2 cans (15 ounces each) chickpeas, rinsed and drained

$^1/_3$ cup nonfat plain Greek yogurt

2 tablespoons extra-virgin olive oil

Juice of $^1/_2$ lemon

4 roasted garlic cloves (page 208)

1 teaspoon ground cumin

1 teaspoon cayenne

2 tablespoons reduced-sodium soy sauce

1 teaspoon sea salt

Dippers

1 jicama, peeled and cut into sticks

1 cucumber, semipeeled (so it's striped) and cut into sticks

1 zucchini, cut into sticks

1 cup grape tomatoes

1 large apple, cut into wedges

1 red bell pepper, cut into strips

1 cup broccoli florets

1 cup cauliflower florets

To make the hummus: Place all of the ingredients in a food processor and blend until smooth. Transfer to a medium bowl and surround with a selection of raw veggie dippers.

Per serving: 138 calories, 3 g fat (0.5 g saturated, 0 g trans), 5 g protein, 9 g fiber, 6 g sugars, 404 mg sodium, 23 g carbohydrates, 0 mg cholesterol

♥ Frugal & Fab

Whether you call them chickpeas or garbanzo beans, you should definitely be calling on them for a diet rich in filling fiber and good protein. I use these little guys on their own or to stretch a salad and bulk up a soup. At just $1 per can (on average), you can't go wrong.

Back in the day, spinach-artichoke dip was my absolute party must-have. After making it dozens of times (always loaded with full-fat mayo and cream cheese), I vowed to come up with a healthier version. It took a few tries, but this skinny version is so right-on that I swear, no one can tell the difference. It's extra fabulous if you let it chill in the fridge overnight. FWB: Garlic, spinach

Hot-Stuff Spinach-Artichoke Dip

SERVES **12**

2 tablespoons extra-virgin olive oil

1 yellow onion, finely chopped

4 garlic cloves, minced

2 cans (14 ounces each) water-packed artichoke hearts, drained, rinsed, and thinly sliced

1 bunch fresh spinach or baby spinach (about 5 ounces), coarsely chopped

8 ounces ⅓-less-fat Neufchâtel cream cheese, at room temperature

1 cup light mayonnaise

⅓ cup (about 2 ounces) grated Parmesan cheese

1 large baguette, cut on the diagonal into ½-inch-thick slices and toasted

Adjust one oven rack to the upper-middle position and keep one rack at the middle position. Preheat the oven to 375°F. Coat an 8-inch baking dish with cooking spray.

Heat 1 tablespoon of the olive oil in a medium nonstick skillet over medium-low heat. Add the onion and garlic and cook until the onion is sticky and golden brown, about 3 minutes, stirring often. Add the artichoke hearts and a few cups of the spinach, turning the mixture over until the spinach leaves wilt. Add the remaining spinach and continue to cook until all the leaves are wilted, about 5 minutes. Set aside to cool.

Stir the cream cheese, mayonnaise, and ¼ cup of the Parmesan together in a large bowl until creamy. Add the cooled spinach mixture and stir to combine. Scrape the mixture into the baking dish and sprinkle with the remaining Parmesan. Bake until the Parmesan is golden brown, about 30 minutes.

Serve with the toasted baguette slices and a clear conscience!

Per serving: 286 calories, 14 g fat (5 g saturated, 0 g trans), 9 g protein, 2 g fiber, 1 g sugars, 847 mg sodium, 29 g carbohydrates, 24 mg cholesterol

Kung-fu kick your bad-for-you Chinese chicken salad habit once and for all. I trade in Asian almonds and sesame seeds for fried wontons, and grill the chicken instead of frying it. Plus, the dressing is fresh and fabulous, not goopy and heavy. This makes a nice lunch for four, too; crumble the wontons on top of the salad for a nice crunch. FWB: Cabbage

Chinese Chicken Salad Chop Cups

MAKES **48** MINI CUPS

Dressing

$\frac{1}{2}$ teaspoon sesame seeds

2 tablespoons plus $\frac{1}{2}$ teaspoon rice vinegar

1 tablespoon reduced-sodium soy sauce

$1\frac{1}{2}$ teaspoons dark sesame oil

$1\frac{1}{2}$ teaspoons honey

1 teaspoon grated fresh ginger

1 tablespoon creamy peanut butter

Salad

1 large boneless, skinless chicken breast (about 8 ounces)

$1\frac{1}{2}$ teaspoons sea salt

$\frac{1}{4}$ teaspoon ground black pepper

48 wonton wrappers

Dark sesame oil

$1\frac{1}{2}$ cups chopped napa cabbage

$1\frac{1}{2}$ cups finely chopped red cabbage

1 medium carrot, coarsely grated

4 scallions, thinly sliced

$\frac{1}{3}$ cup finely chopped cilantro

$\frac{1}{4}$ cup Asian Almonds (page 55)

To make the dressing: Place the sesame seeds in a small skillet over medium heat and toast, shaking the pan often, until they're fragrant and golden, about 2 minutes. Transfer the sesame seeds to a medium bowl. Add the vinegar, soy sauce, sesame oil, honey, and ginger and whisk to combine. Add the peanut butter and whisk until completely smooth. Set aside.

To make the salad: Preheat the oven to 350°F. Heat a ridged cast iron grill pan over medium-high heat for 2 minutes. Lightly coat with cooking spray. Season the chicken with $\frac{1}{2}$ teaspoon of the salt and the pepper and grill until both sides have grill marks and the chicken is cooked through, 10 to 15 minutes. Set aside until cool.

Press 1 wonton wrapper into each cup of a 24-cup nonstick mini muffin pan (the ends will peek up above the cups). Brush with a little sesame oil and sprinkle with $\frac{1}{2}$ teaspoon of the salt. Bake until golden brown and crisp, 5 to 7 minutes. Remove from the oven and set aside to cool for 5 minutes before gently lifting the wonton cups out of the pan. Repeat with the remaining wonton wrappers, sesame oil, and $\frac{1}{2}$ teaspoon salt.

Chop the chicken into $\frac{1}{2}$-inch cubes. Place them in a large bowl and add the cabbages, carrot, scallions, and cilantro. Toss with

(continued)

three-fourths of the dressing. Fill each wonton cup with 1 heaping tablespoon of salad and top with the Asian Almonds and extra cilantro. Serve immediately with the remaining dressing on the side.

Per mini cup: 45 calories, 1.5 g fat (0 g saturated, 0 g trans), 3 g protein, 0.5 g fiber, <1 g sugars, 124 mg sodium, 6 g carbohydrates, 3 mg cholesterol

↓ Slim Scoop!

When you make salad, don't go bonkers with the dressing. Save a little to serve on the side—this keeps things light and lets your friends do up their salads with as much or as little dressing as they like. The salad and wonton cups can be made a few hours ahead of time, just hold back on filling the wonton cups until right before serving so they stay nice and crisp.

I find myself munching on a handful of these savory almonds whenever I start craving something salty and naughty. These make a great topping for salads, so I often bag them up for lunchtime. FWB: Almonds

Asian Almonds

MAKES **1** CUP

2 tablespoons reduced-sodium soy sauce

2 teaspoons dark sesame oil

$\frac{1}{2}$ teaspoon cayenne

$\frac{1}{2}$ teaspoon garlic powder

$\frac{1}{2}$ teaspoon ground ginger

1 cup sliced almonds (about 3 ounces)

Preheat the oven to 375°F. Line a rimmed baking sheet with parchment paper. Whisk the soy sauce, sesame oil, cayenne, garlic powder, and ginger together in a medium bowl. Add the almonds and toss gently to coat them with the mixture (try not to break them—they're so pretty whole!). Spread on the baking sheet and roast until browned and crisp, about 10 minutes. Cool completely before transferring to an airtight container. Store at room temperature for up to 2 weeks.

Per tablespoon: 40 calories, 3.5 g fat (0.5 g saturated, 0 g trans), 1 g protein, 1 g fiber, 0 g sugars, 72 mg sodium, 2 g carbohydrates, 0 mg cholesterol

♡ Frugal & Fab

For a great price on nuts, check out the bulk bins in natural foods stores (they usually have frequent turnover too, so your nuts will be ultra fresh), warehouse stores, and ethnic markets.

Cooked shrimp ceviche is healthy, fresh, and fast, involving just a little chopping and a few squeezes of citrus. It takes about as much effort to make as homemade salsa but it's way more hip and classy. Scooped into endive "boats," ceviche is the perfect three-bite snack that will leave you feeling comfortably satisfied and smiling. FWB: Avocado, bell pepper

Shrimp and Avocado Ceviche Dream Boats

MAKES **40** ENDIVE BOATS

1 pound cooked medium shrimp, finely chopped

1 red bell pepper, chopped

½ small red onion, finely chopped

1 small cucumber, halved, seeded, and finely chopped

¼ cup fresh lemon juice (1–2 lemons)

¼ cup fresh lime juice (2 limes)

½ cup plus 2 tablespoons finely chopped cilantro

1 tablespoon chili powder

¼ teaspoon sea salt

4 large endive, separated into leaves (you should have about 40 total)

1 semi-ripe Hass avocado, finely chopped

Place the chopped shrimp in a large glass or plastic bowl (metal can react with the citrus juices). Add the bell pepper, onion, and cucumber and stir together. Add the lemon and lime juices, ½ cup of the cilantro, the chili powder, and salt and stir to combine. Cover with plastic wrap and refrigerate for at least 15 minutes or up to 30 minutes.

Set the endive spears on a work surface. Gently stir the avocado into the ceviche. Fill each endive spear with 1 tablespoon of the mixture. Place the endive boats on a platter, sprinkle with the remaining 2 tablespoons cilantro, and serve.

Per endive boat: 20 calories, 1 g fat (0 g saturated, 0 g trans), 3 g protein, 0.5 g fiber, 0 g sugars, 36 mg sodium, 1 g carbohydrates, 22 mg cholesterol

♥ Frugal & Fab

Save a few dollars by cleaning and cooking your own shrimp. Buy medium 26/30 count shrimp (meaning you get 26 to 30 shrimp in a pound), remove the shells and the veins, then quickly poach them in water seasoned with a pinch of salt and a squeeze of lemon or lime juice. You know they're done the moment they start to curl—drain them immediately and plunge into ice water for perfectly tender little tasty bites.

🟢 = vegetarian   🟢 = vegan

CHAPTER 3

Soups & Salads

Once upon time, some moron thought it would be a great idea to add bacon, fried onion rings, fried croutons, gobs of cheese, and mounds of ranch dressing to a beautiful bowl of healthy greens and veggies—and then had the nerve to call it "salad"! Who was that person kidding? And speaking of a million hidden calories and fat grams, what about soup loaded with cream and cheese (broccoli-Cheddar soup anyone? Have you ever seen the fat content on lobster bisque?). Soups and salads should be vibrant and fresh, full of color and nutrients, not calories, cholesterol, and fat. I'm all for bringing that simple beauty back. Come on and jump on the fresh bandwagon!

Did you know that a popular dining chain I'll call Restaurant X has a Caesar on its menu that weighs in at 600 calories and 43 (yes, 43!) grams of fat? That's nearly 123 percent of your daily upper limit! Ridiculously insane, right? Though Caesar is a classic, even classics can stand updating now and again—and this is definitely one of those times. FWB: Nonfat yogurt, apples

The Skinny Caesar

SERVES **4**

Croutons

1/2 whole wheat baguette

1 tablespoon extra-virgin olive oil

1/4 teaspoon garlic powder

Dressing

1/4 cup nonfat plain Greek yogurt

2 tablespoons extra-virgin olive oil

2 tablespoons Dijon mustard

1 tablespoon balsamic vinegar

1 teaspoon fresh lemon juice

1 garlic clove, finely minced

1/2 teaspoon ground black pepper

Salad

2 romaine lettuce hearts

1 can (14 ounces) hearts of palm, rinsed and thinly sliced crosswise

1/2 Fuji apple, thinly sliced

1/2 cup Asian Almonds (page 55)

2 tablespoons grated Parmesan

To make the croutons: Preheat the oven to 375°F. Slice the baguette on the diagonal into 1/4-inch-thick slices. Place the bread slices on a rimmed baking sheet and brush one side with the olive oil. Sprinkle with the salt and garlic powder and bake until both sides are golden brown, about 12 minutes total, turning the croutons over midway through. Set aside to cool.

To make the dressing: Whisk the yogurt, oil, mustard, vinegar, lemon juice, garlic, pepper, and salt together in a large salad bowl.

To assemble the salad: Separate the romaine into individual leaves. Add the lettuce, hearts of palm, and apple to the salad bowl and toss to coat with the dressing. Top with the croutons and almonds and finish with the Parmesan.

Per serving: 414 calories, 18 g fat (3 g saturated, 0 g trans), 12 g protein, 8 g fiber, 5 g sugars, 917 mg sodium, 55 g carbohydrates, 2 mg cholesterol

♥Frugal & Fab

You know the bread ends and heels you're always throwing away? They're perfect for turning into croutons and bread crumbs. So cube leftover bread and save it in a gallon-size resealable freezer bag, toss with a little oil and salt, and toast in the oven for a crunchy freebie.

Who says that you have to go to fancy restaurant to have a "gourmet" meal? Serve this salad in small portions on salad plates rather than family-style in a large bowl to get that fine dining feel for a fraction of the price! Bonus: You get to control the quantity and quality of every ingredient that goes onto your plate. FWB: Asparagus

Asparagus Ribbon, Sweet Corn, and Cress with Pom Vinaigrette

SERVES 4

Vinaigrette

2 tablespoons balsamic vinegar

1 teaspoon Dijon mustard

$1/2$ teaspoon sea salt

$1/4$ cup pure pomegranate juice

2 teaspoons extra-virgin olive oil

Salad

1 bunch watercress, thick stems discarded

1 pound asparagus, tough ends snapped off

$1/4$ cup corn kernels—fresh, frozen (thawed) or canned (rinsed)

To make the vinaigrette: Whisk the vinegar, mustard, and salt together in a small bowl. Add the pomegranate juice and olive oil and whisk to combine. Set aside.

To make the salads: Divide the watercress among plates. Using a vegetable peeler, shave the asparagus spears into thin ribbons and add some to each serving. Top with the corn and sprinkle lightly with some of the vinaigrette (save some to pass at the table).

Per serving: 65 calories, 3 g fat (0.5 g saturated, 0 g trans), 3 g protein, 2 g fiber, 5 g sugars, 239 mg sodium, 9 g carbohydrates, 0 mg cholesterol

♡ Frugal & Fab

Asparagus can be pricey, but it's so high in folate, vitamin C, and potassium that I love to add it to salads. Sometimes I'll just use the stalks in salad and save the tips for a stir-fry or to add to a risotto. Voilà—you just doubled your investment, superstar!

Feel Good Sesame-Cucumber Salad

SERVES **4**

Dressing

¹⁄₄ cup rice vinegar

1 tablespoon dark sesame oil

1 tablespoon reduced-sodium soy sauce

1 tablespoon honey

1 tablespoon sesame seeds

Salad

1 large cucumber, semipeeled (so it's striped), halved lengthwise, and cut into ¹⁄₄-inch-thick slices

1 cup thinly sliced red cabbage (about ¹⁄₈ head)

2 medium carrots, grated on the large holes of a box grater

¹⁄₂ red bell pepper, thinly sliced

2 scallions, thinly sliced on the diagonal

To make the dressing: Whisk the vinegar, sesame oil, soy sauce, and honey together in a large bowl. Place the sesame seeds in a small skillet and cook over medium heat, shaking the pan often, until they are fragrant and toasty, 1 to 2 minutes. Immediately add the hot sesame seeds to the dressing (I love that sizzle sound!).

To make the salad: Add the cucumber, cabbage, carrots, and pepper to the dressing and toss to coat. Let the veggies marinate for 10 minutes, then divide the salad among 4 plates. Sprinkle with the scallions and serve.

Per serving: 95 calories, 5 g fat (0.5 g saturated, 0 g trans), 2 g protein, 2 g fiber, 8 g sugars, 178 mg sodium, 12 g carbohydrates, 0 mg cholesterol

♡ Frugal & Fab

Turn this into a very inexpensive and skinny meal by serving the salad over your favorite greens and adding a few slices of firm tofu splashed with a little soy sauce on the side. Delish!

Turning Over a New Leaf

Tired of the same-old iceberg salad? Try a few of my faves:

Arugula: My absolute #1 pick. Slightly bitter, savory, peppery flavor. Great on pizza, a sandwich, mixed with mild greens for salad, or with the crab cakes on page 139.

Bibb/Boston: Because their leaves are so tender and soft, this type of lettuce is often called butterhead. Sometimes, depending on the season, it can be on the pricey side—if so, just sub red leaf or romaine instead. Great with the Hollywood Burger on page 174!

Endive: Juicy, crunchy quality with a lingering bitter ending. Makes a great guilt-free alternative to chips for dip.

Mizuna: A feathery Japanese green, this is destined to be the next arugula. It has a slight peppery bite.

Radicchio: Gorgeous and vibrant crimson and white leaves with a cabbage-like texture. Watch out—this guy has a bitter edge.

Red leaf: Green at the base with a pretty purple frilled top. Tender enough for vinaigrette but can stand up to a creamy dressing too. Totally delish with blueberries or grilled nectarines.

Romaine: By far the most popular kid in the leafy green class. Use the outer leaves for the Skinny Caesar on page 61. Save the inner ones for hummus and guac dippers!

Tat soi: Another great Asian leafy green that is a cousin to cabbage. It has a great peppery finish and is scrumptious mixed into salads, soups, and stir-fries.

Watercress: Watercress is a member of the mustard family, and it adds a bit of peppery bite to salads. Snap off the thickest stems and use soon after buying, as it is quite perishable.

When I was young I was not the biggest beet fan, but fast-forward 20 years and here I am waving my fuchsia flag! They're sweet, tender, and loaded with nutrients, not to mention that fab hot pink color—what's not to love? If you don't love the pink-stained fingers, then just go for stainless golden beets! This is elegant, simple, and delicious. FWB: Beets

Roasted Beet and Granny Salad

SERVES **4**

Vinaigrette

1½ tablespoons red wine vinegar

1 tablespoon fresh lemon juice

3 tablespoons extra-virgin olive oil

Salad

1½ pounds red or golden beets (about 6 medium)

4 cups arugula

½ Granny Smith apple, thinly sliced

¼ teaspoon sea salt

¼ teaspoon ground black pepper

¼ cup raw hulled pumpkin seeds

To make the vinaigrette: Whisk the vinegar and lemon juice together in a small bowl. Add the olive oil and whisk to combine.

To make the salad: Preheat the oven to 400°F. Wrap each beet in a square of foil making sure the entire beet is enclosed. Place the wrapped beets on a rimmed baking sheet and roast until a paring knife easily slides into the center of the largest one, 1 hour to 1 hour 15 minutes (possibly longer if you're using large beets). Set aside to cool, then unwrap, peel, and cut into ⅛-inch-thick rounds.

Place the arugula and apple in a medium bowl along with half of the vinaigrette, the salt, and pepper and toss to coat. Divide the salad mixture among 4 plates. Place the beets in the bowl along with half of the remaining vinaigrette and toss to coat. Arrange the beets on top of the greens and sprinkle with the pumpkin seeds.

Per serving: 227 calories, 15 g fat (2 g saturated, 0 g trans), 5 g protein, 6 g fiber, 14 g sugars, 238 mg sodium, 21 g carbohydrates, 0 mg cholesterol

♡ Frugal & Fab

Don't you think for one second about throwing away those gorgeous leafy green beet tops! Sauté them with a few splashes of olive oil, some thinly sliced garlic, salt, and pepper, or pack the chopped raw greens with rice vinegar and salt and pepper overnight in the fridge.

Whenever I fall into a salad rut, I grill some fruit, drop it on top of the greens, and just like that, my salad goes from tired to amazing! Try swapping out your tomatoes or cucumbers for some nectarines, peaches, or plums; or toss in a handful of sliced strawberries or blueberries instead of cheese or deli ham or turkey. Candied Walnuts (page 74) are decadently delicious sprinkled on top (in moderation of course). FWB: Nectarines

Grilled Nectarine Salad with Blue Cheese Crumbles

SERVES 4

Vinaigrette

¼ cup champagne vinegar

1 tablespoon fresh orange juice

1½ teaspoons Dijon mustard

¼ teaspoon sea salt

1½ teaspoons extra-virgin olive oil

Salad

Extra-virgin olive oil

3 nectarines, halved

¼ teaspoon sea salt

4 cups salad greens (torn red leaf, baby spinach, or baby arugula)

¼ cup (1 ounce) crumbled blue cheese

To make the vinaigrette: Whisk the vinegar, orange juice, mustard, and salt together in a small bowl. Add the olive oil and whisk to combine.

To make the salad: Heat a ridged cast iron grill pan over medium-high heat (or heat a grill to medium-high). Using tongs, dip a paper towel into a little olive oil and use it to oil the grill pan (or grill grates). Brush the cut-side of the nectarine halves lightly with olive oil and sprinkle with the salt. Grill cut-side down until they have grill marks and take on a juicy, golden look, about 3 minutes. Remove from the grill and set aside to cool, then thinly slice.

Toss the salad greens with the sliced nectarines. Add three-fourths of the vinaigrette and toss to coat. Divide the salad among 4 plates, sprinkle with the cheese, and serve the remaining vinaigrette on the side.

Per serving: 141 calories, 8 g fat (2 g saturated, 0 g trans), 4 g protein, 3 g fiber, 9 g sugars, 373 mg sodium, 15 g carbohydrates, 6 mg cholesterol

Slim Scoop!

At 5 measly calories per teaspoon, you can't beat Dijon mustard! It adds a great creaminess to thin vinaigrettes and a wonderful spicy tang with hardly any calories or fat, so stock up.

When flavors come together in such perfect harmony as these do, I fall in love from the very first bite. The combo of tart strawberries, crunchy walnuts, and salty cheese just does it for me! It's even more fabulous when tossed with my homemade zero-fat (yep, zero) balsamic vinaigrette. FWB: Walnuts, spinach

Spinach Salad with Walnuts and Strawberries

SERVES **4**

½ cup walnuts

4 cups fresh baby spinach, stems trimmed, coarsely chopped

8 large strawberries, thinly sliced

¼ cup balsamic vinegar

3 tablespoons honey

2 tablespoons spicy brown mustard

¼ teaspoon sea salt

¼ cup (1 ounce) crumbled feta (optional)

Preheat the oven to 375°F. Place the walnuts on a rimmed baking sheet and bake until fragrant and toasted, about 8 minutes. Transfer to a plate to cool.

Toss the spinach with the strawberries in a large bowl. Whisk together the vinegar, honey, mustard, and salt in a small bowl. Drizzle three-fourths of the dressing over the salad and sprinkle the walnuts on top. Serve sprinkled with cheese, if desired, and with the remaining dressing on the side.

Per serving: 172 calories, 8 g fat (1 g saturated, 0 g trans), 3 g protein, 3 g fiber, 17 g sugars, 217 mg sodium, 23 g carbohydrates, 0 mg cholesterol

As a kid, biting into a giant smiley wedge of watermelon always managed to turn an ordinary day into something special. While my carefree days of watermelon juice dripping from my chin might be behind me, I still get that watermelon face smile every time I make this simple, easy, classy salad. FWB: Watermelon

Watermelon and Feta with a Balsamic Reduction

SERVES 4

2 cups balsamic vinegar

1 baby seedless watermelon, ½ small seedless watermelon, or 4 cups seeded watermelon chunks

½ cup small fresh basil leaves or torn larger leaves

½ cup (2 ounces) crumbled feta cheese

Heat the balsamic vinegar in a small saucepan over medium-high heat until it comes to a gentle boil. Reduce the heat to medium and simmer until the balsamic is reduced to about ¾ cup and has the consistency of maple syrup, about 30 minutes. Cool to room temperature.

If using uncut watermelon, halve it. Trim the rind from the watermelon halves (or half) and cut the melon into ¼-inch-thick slices.

Divide the watermelon slices or chunks among 4 plates. Sprinkle with the basil and then drizzle some of the balsamic reduction over each plate. Top with the crumbled feta and serve.

Per serving: 197 calories, 3 g fat (2 g saturated, 0 g trans), 4 g protein, 1 g fiber, 29 g sugars, 189 mg sodium, 34 g carbohydrates, 13 mg cholesterol

I whip out these candied walnuts when I want to add a special sweet-crunchy bite to a salad, especially those with sharp cheese or fruit. They are also fantastic served alongside a martini. They keep really well, too. They're filling and loaded with omega-3s, but be sure to use your judgment when eating them—they're dangerous to the waistline if downed by the handful. FWB: Walnuts

Candice's Candied Walnuts

MAKES **2¼** CUPS

⅓ cup granulated sugar

2 tablespoons light brown sugar

½ teaspoon ground cinnamon

½ teaspoon sea salt

1 egg white, at room temperature

8 ounces walnut halves
  (about 2 heaping cups)

Preheat the oven to 350°F. Line a rimmed baking sheet with parchment paper. Stir the sugars, cinnamon, and salt together in a small bowl and set aside.

Whisk the egg white in a medium bowl until frothy, then whisk in 1 tablespoon of warm water. Stir in the walnuts making sure the egg white mixture coats them well, getting into all of the cracks. Add the spiced sugar and toss to coat. Spread the walnuts in an even layer on the baking sheet and bake until toasted, crisp, and caramelized, about 20 minutes; stir after about 12 minutes (don't worry if some of the coating sticks to the parchment). Let the nuts cool on the pan, then store in an airtight container at room temperature for up to 3 months.

Per ¼ cup: 228 calories, 18 g fat (2 g saturated, 0 g trans), 5 g protein, 2 g fiber, 11 g sugars, 705 mg sodium, 15 g carbohydrates, 0 mg cholesterol

After traveling to Paris, I fell in love—not with the fashion, the men, or the vino, but with tuna Niçoise! I relive the memories by making this protein-packed salad. The honey–red wine vinaigrette gives the salad a tinge of sweetness that I love, especially with a nice glass of chilled wine. FWB: Tuna, beans

3-Bean Tuna Niçoise

SERVES 4

Vinaigrette

2 tablespoons red wine vinegar

1 tablespoon Dijon mustard

1 teaspoon honey

½ teaspoon sea salt

2 tablespoons extra-virgin olive oil

Salad

2 large eggs

1 cup green beans

¾ teaspoon sea salt

1 head romaine lettuce, tough outer leaves removed, inner leaves thinly sliced crosswise

½ cup canned chickpeas, rinsed and drained

½ cup canned kidney beans, rinsed and drained

2 Roma tomatoes, thinly sliced lengthwise

1 can (5 ounces) water-packed albacore tuna, drained

To make the vinaigrette: Whisk the vinegar, mustard, honey, and salt together in a small bowl. Whisk in the olive oil.

To make the salad: Place the eggs in a medium saucepan and cover with water. Bring the water to a boil over medium-high heat, turn off the heat, cover the pan, and set aside for 10 minutes. Remove the eggs and place them in a bowl of cold water until they're cool enough to peel. Peel, quarter lengthwise, and set aside.

Fill a medium saucepan with 1 inch of water. Place a steamer insert in the pot and bring the water to a simmer over high heat. Add the green beans, sprinkle with ¼ teaspoon of the salt, reduce the heat to low, cover, and steam until tender, 6 to 8 minutes. Rinse the beans under cold water to stop the cooking, drain, and set aside.

Divide the lettuce, chickpeas, kidney beans, and tomatoes among 4 shallow bowls. Top each serving with one-fourth of the tuna and 2 egg quarters. Arrange the green beans on top.

Drizzle the dressing over the salads and sprinkle each serving with some of the remaining ½ teaspoon salt. Serve.

Per serving: 223 calories, 11 g fat (2 g saturated, 0 g trans), 15 g protein, 5 g fiber, 4 g sugars, 898 mg sodium, 17 g carbohydrates, 118 mg cholesterol

As a kid I was totally addicted to California Pizza Kitchen's insanely yummy barbecue chicken chopped salad. Little did I know that my favorite everything-but-the-kitchen-sink salad was costing me more than 1,100 calories and 16 grams of saturated fat! Rather than swear off my favorite guilty pleasure entirely, I created a killer faux ranch dressing that gives CPK's a run for its money but gives me a lot less baggage to carry around. FWB: Avocado

BBQ-Ranch Chicken Chop Salad

SERVES 4

1 teaspoon canola or vegetable oil

2 links chicken sausage

¼ cup store-bought or homemade barbecue sauce (page 176)

¼ cup nonfat plain Greek yogurt

1 romaine lettuce heart, finely chopped

1 cup canned chickpeas, rinsed and drained

½ small red onion, very finely chopped

½ cup finely chopped cilantro

1 large tomato (preferably beefsteak), finely chopped

1 Hass avocado, finely diced

½ teaspoon sea salt (optional)

Heat the oil in a small nonstick skillet (or coat with cooking spray) over medium heat for 1 minute. Add the chicken sausage and brown on all sides, 6 to 8 minutes total. Set aside to cool, then thinly slice.

Whisk the barbecue sauce and yogurt together in a small bowl.

Toss the lettuce, chickpeas, red onion, and cilantro together in a large bowl. Add three-fourths of the yogurt dressing and toss to coat. Turn the chickpea mixture out onto a large platter and spread out evenly. Arrange the chicken sausage, avocado, and tomato in 3 stripes over the lettuce mixture (like a Cobb). Sprinkle with the salt, if desired, and serve.

Per serving: 230 calories, 12 g fat (2 g saturated, 0 g trans), 11 g protein, 7 g fiber, 8 g sugars, 636 mg sodium, 23 g carbohydrates, 33 mg cholesterol

When I was a kid, I spent a few months in Japan and always thought it was so cool how we ate miso soup for breakfast! It was warm and comforting and felt so good to sip first thing in the morning. My love affair with miso paste has been going strong ever since. I use it as a condiment to give body and a savory umami quality to all kinds of sauces and dressings. FWB: Miso

Miso Fabulous Soup and Salad Combo

SERVES **4**

Miso soup

3 tablespoons miso paste (see So Many Miso, page 145)

1 cup firm tofu cubes (about ½ of a 14-ounce package)

5 scallions, thinly sliced on the diagonal

Miso salad

2 tablespoons light mayonnaise

1 tablespoon miso paste (preferably red)

1 tablespoon rice vinegar

1 head tender lettuce (like Bibb or Boston; about 4 cups)

1 large carrot, grated on the large holes of a box grater

1 small cucumber, semipeeled (so it's striped), halved lengthwise, and sliced crosswise

1 Hass avocado, thinly sliced

1 package (14 ounces) firm tofu, cut into cubes

2 tablespoons Asian Almonds (page 55), optional

To make the soup: Bring 4 cups of water to a boil in a medium saucepan. Whisk in the miso and reduce the heat to medium-low. Simmer the soup gently (don't boil) for 5 minutes and then add the tofu cubes and turn off the heat. Cover to keep warm while you make the salad.

To make the salad: Whisk the mayonnaise, miso paste, and vinegar together in a small bowl. Toss the lettuce with the carrot and cucumber in a large bowl. Divide the salad among 4 plates. Top with a few avocado slices, a few pieces of tofu, and Asian Almonds, if desired, and drizzle with some dressing.

Divide the soup among 4 bowls and sprinkle with the scallions. Serve both for a killer soup and salad combo!

Per serving: 262 calories, 14.5 g fat (2 g saturated, 0 g trans), 15 g protein, 8 g fiber, 6 g sugars, 718 mg sodium, 18 g carbohydrates, 3 mg cholesterol

♥ Frugal & Fab
You can usually find miso in the produce section of the supermarket at around $5 a container. A little goes a really long way, so it's worth every penny!

Whether I'm in LA or NYC, this cream-free yet creamy soup immediately transports me to the country, to changing leaves and pumpkin patches and the whole autumn deal. The rich-tasting duo of naturally buttery squash and sweet Fuji apples tastes like a million bucks. And the finishing drizzle of real maple syrup is totally decadent—like adding a kiss of velvet. FWB: Butternut squash

Creamy Butternut Squash and Apple Soup

SERVES 4

2 tablespoons unsalted butter

I onion, coarsely chopped

1¾ pounds butternut squash, peeled, halved, seeded, and cut into I-inch chunks (about 5 cups)

2 apples (like Fuji), coarsely chopped

4 cups low-sodium chicken broth

I cup unsweetened almond milk

2 tablespoons maple syrup

I teaspoon pumpkin pie spice plus extra for serving

Nonfat Greek yogurt for serving (optional)

Melt the butter in a large soup pot over medium heat. Add the onion and cook until caramelized, stirring often, about 10 minutes. Add the squash and apples and cook until browned on all sides, stirring occasionally, until golden brown, about 15 minutes. Add 3½ cups of the chicken broth and bring to a boil. Reduce the heat to medium and simmer until the apples and squash are tender, about 20 minutes, stirring often to make sure the squash doesn't stick to the bottom of the pot.

Transfer some of the soup to a blender (don't fill the blender more than two-thirds full with hot soup, otherwise the steam will force the lid off and you'll have a butternut mess on your walls!). Add ¼ cup of the almond milk, the maple syrup, and pumpkin pie spice. Pulse to release some heat, and then blend until smooth. Pour the soup into a clean pot and repeat with the remaining soup and remaining almond milk, dividing it into 2 or 3 batches (so you don't overfill the blender) if necessary. If the soup looks too thick, add up to ½ cup of the remaining chicken broth. Heat the soup until warmed through and serve. I love it with a dollop of yogurt and extra pie spice sprinkled over the top.

Per serving: 241 calories, 7 g fat (4 g saturated, 0 g trans), 5 g protein, 3 g fiber, 8 g sugars, 513 mg sodium, 13 g carbohydrates, 0 mg cholesterol

If you're thinking that homemade soup is too time-consuming and sounds like too much work, then you absolutely must make this protein-loaded asparagus soup. Just brown some onions and garlic, and then throw a bunch of ingredients into a pot and voilà, you're donezo. Unlike opening a can, you get to control the calories, sodium, and, most important, the flavor! FWB: Asparagus

Quick and Easy Asparagus-Chickpea Soup

SERVES 4

1 tablespoon extra-virgin olive oil or canola oil

1 onion, halved and thinly sliced

6 garlic cloves, smashed with the side of a chef's knife

1 can (15 ounces) chickpeas, rinsed and drained

4 cups low-sodium chicken broth

2 tablespoons reduced-sodium soy sauce

1/4 teaspoon sea salt

1/4 teaspoon ground black pepper

1 pound asparagus, cut on the diagonal into 1/2-inch pieces

2 tablespoons grated Parmesan cheese

1 tablespoon finely chopped fresh basil (optional)

Heat the oil in a large soup pot over medium-high heat. Add the onion and garlic, reduce the heat to medium-low, and cook until the onion is golden brown and caramelized, about 20 minutes, stirring often. Sprinkle the pan with a tablespoon or two of water if the onions begin to stick to the bottom.

Add the chickpeas and chicken broth and bring to a boil. Reduce the heat to medium and add the soy sauce, salt, and pepper. Simmer for 3 minutes. Add the asparagus and cook until the asparagus is tender, about 2 minutes. Turn off the heat and serve sprinkled with the Parmesan and basil, if desired.

___

Per serving: 174 calories, 5.5 g fat (1 g saturated, 0 g trans), 10 g protein, 6 g fiber, 6 g sugars, 584 mg sodium, 22 g carbohydrates, 2 mg cholesterol

♡ Frugal & Fab

Divide leftover soup into small freezer-friendly plastic containers. Presto, you have a healthy lunch or light dinner ready to go whenever you need it—and so much healthier than a pizza!

I grew up on delicious buckwheat soba noodles. We ate them with everything from a simple miso broth (page 79) to tofu, fish, and veggies. Soba is still one of my favorites because it's gluten free (see Slim Scoop, below), high in protein, and also has calcium and iron. You can't get that from any old pasta! Buy two packs of noodles: Save one for this soup and use the others with my yummy peanut sauce on page 163. Heaven! FWB: Soba noodles

Soba Noodle Soup

SERVES 4

8 ounces soba noodles

1 teaspoon sea salt

4 cups low-sodium chicken broth

2 tablespoons reduced-sodium soy sauce

3 garlic cloves, finely minced

2 teaspoons grated fresh ginger

7 dried shiitake mushrooms, covered in boiling water 5 minutes, drained, and chopped

4 scallions, thinly sliced on the diagonal

1 cup chopped baby spinach leaves

2 hard-cooked eggs, peeled and halved (optional)

Bring a large pot of water to a boil. Add the soba noodles and the salt and cook until the noodles are cooked through, 2 to 3 minutes. Drain in a medium-mesh sieve and rinse the noodles under cold running water for 1 minute.

Meanwhile, make the soup. Bring the chicken broth, soy sauce, garlic, and ginger to a boil in a large saucepan over high heat. Reduce the heat to medium and simmer for 3 minutes, then add the mushrooms and simmer until they're tender, about 5 minutes. Add three-fourths of the scallions and simmer until soft, about 1 minute.

Divide the noodles among 4 bowls and pour the soup over the noodles. Add the spinach, sprinkle with the remaining scallions, and serve each bowl with a hard-cooked egg half, if desired. Kampai!

Per serving: 250 calories, 1 g fat (0 g saturated, 0 g trans), 10 g protein, 4 g fiber, 3 g sugars, 469 mg sodium, 52 g carbohydrates, 0 mg cholesterol

Slim Scoop!

If you're gluten intolerant or are making soba noodles for someone who is, be sure to read the ingredient list on the package. Sometimes wheat flour is mixed in with the buckwheat flour.

Start to finish, you can have this incredibly dreamy, creamy (thanks to cream-less nonfat yogurt!), velvety-smooth tomato soup served up in 30 minutes! It's wonderful for dinner—just the remedy for a cold winter night. I love it with the Totally Un-Croque Monsieur Fingers (page 39). FWB: Tomatoes

"Creamy" Tomato Soup

SERVES 4

1 tablespoon canola oil

1 small yellow onion, finely chopped

2 garlic cloves, very finely minced

1 sprig fresh sage or 2 teaspoons dried sage

1 sprig fresh thyme or 2 teaspoons dried thyme

4 tablespoons tomato paste

1 can (28 ounces) low-sodium diced tomatoes

$\frac{1}{2}$ cup low-sodium chicken broth

$\frac{1}{2}$ cup unsweetened almond milk

$\frac{1}{4}$ cup nonfat plain Greek yogurt plus extra for serving

1 teaspoon sea salt

3 tablespoons finely chopped fresh basil (optional)

Heat the oil in a large saucepan over medium-high heat. Add the onion, garlic, sage, and thyme. Reduce the heat to medium-low and cook, stirring occasionally, until the mixture is soft and fragrant, about 3 minutes.

Stir in the tomato paste and cook, stirring constantly, until the tomato paste darkens, $1\frac{1}{2}$ to 2 minutes. Add the canned tomatoes (and their juices) and simmer, stirring occasionally, until slightly thickened and reduced, about 7 minutes. Remove the sage and thyme sprigs and discard. Transfer the mixture to a food processor and pulse to combine. Add the chicken broth, almond milk, and yogurt and process until completely smooth.

Pour the soup back into a clean pot and cook over medium heat until it's warm, about 5 minutes. Stir in the sea salt. Serve with a dollop of yogurt and some chopped fresh basil (if you have some in the fridge).

Per serving: 110 calories, 4 g fat (0 g saturated, 0 g trans), 5 g protein, 3 g fiber, 8 g sugars, 513 mg sodium, 13 g carbohydrates, 0 mg cholesterol

Whenever I roast a chicken, after carving away all of the meat, I save the cooked frame (yep, that's the carcass!) for making this soup—or just the broth, which I freeze for making soup another time. It's totally old-school, but hey, it avoids waste and keeps money in your wallet! What isn't fabulous about that? This is a fantastic recipe for day-after-Thanksgiving turkey soup, too. FWB: Greens

Heartwarming Chicken Soup

SERVES 6

Broth

1 tablespoon canola or extra-virgin olive oil

3 medium carrots, coarsely chopped

2 celery stalks, coarsely chopped

1 onion, coarsely chopped

Carcass from a roasted or rotisserie chicken or ½ of a roasted turkey

Soup

1 tablespoon canola oil

2 medium carrots, cut crosswise into ¼-inch slices

1 celery stalk, thinly sliced

½ small yellow onion, finely chopped

2 teaspoons plus 1 tablespoon sea salt

1 teaspoon ground black pepper

2 cups shredded leftover cooked chicken (optional)

1 cup coarsely chopped mizuna leaves or collard greens

2 cups small bite-size whole grain pasta like macaroni, shells, or orzo

To make the broth: Heat the oil in a large pot over medium-high heat. Add the carrots, celery, and onion. Reduce the heat to medium-low and cook, stirring often, until they're soft and fragrant but not browned, about 7 minutes.

Add the carcass and cook to heat through, stirring often, about 2 minutes. Add 5 cups of water to the pot (it should cover the bones) and bring to a boil. Reduce the heat to medium-low. Simmer until the broth is a rich yellow color, about 45 minutes, skimming off any foam that rises to the surface. Strain through a mesh sieve. Discard the solids. Clean out the pot to make the soup.

To make the soup: Heat the oil in the pot over medium-high heat. Add the carrots, celery, onion, 2 teaspoons of the salt, and the pepper. Reduce the heat to medium and cook, stirring often, until the carrots are just tender, about 10 minutes. Add the strained broth, shredded chicken (if desired), and mizuna. Taste for seasoning, adding salt and pepper if necessary. Set aside.

Bring a large pot of water to a boil. Add the remaining 1 tablespoon salt and the pasta and cook just until al dente. Drain and divide the pasta among 4 bowls. Ladle some soup into each bowl and serve.

Per serving: 215 calories, 5 g fat (1 g saturated, 0 g trans), 10 g protein, 4 g fiber, 4 g sugars, 856 mg sodium, 35 g carbohydrates, 5 mg cholesterol

Who says ramen is just for college students and starving artists? I swear, I could live on this soup! It's quick, delicious, and light. I buy those cheap packages of ramen noodle soup, ditch the spice packet (they're loaded with sodium and other gross ingredients) and add fresh leafy greens, bean sprouts, and shrimp to bulk it up. FWB: Greens

Shrimp and Veggie Ramen

SERVES **4**

2 teaspoons canola oil

1 small yellow onion, halved and thinly sliced

4 cups low-sodium chicken or vegetable broth

1–2 tablespoons reduced-sodium soy sauce

2 cups collard or mustard greens, chopped

1 package (3 ounces) ramen noodle soup, seasoning packet discarded

8 ounces medium shrimp, peeled and deveined

1 cup bean sprouts

Dark sesame oil for serving (optional)

Chili oil for serving (optional)

Heat the canola oil in a medium pot over medium heat. Add the onion and cook, stirring often, until soft and translucent, about 5 minutes. Add the broth and 1 tablespoon of soy sauce, increase the heat to high, and bring to a simmer. Add the greens and cook for 1 minute. Add the ramen and cook for 1 minute. Add the shrimp and simmer until the shrimp are opaque and the ramen is cooked, 2 or 3 minutes longer. Taste for seasoning, adding more soy sauce if needed. Serve topped with bean sprouts and, if desired, a drizzle of sesame and/or chili oil.

Per serving: 206 calories, 5 g fat (1 g saturated, 0 g trans), 20 g protein, 3 g fiber, 3 g sugars, 386 mg sodium, 22 g carbohydrates, 86 mg cholesterol

Slim Scoop!

In many cases, instant ramen noodles aren't as innocent as you think. Some are flash-fried and contain palm and cottonseed oils. Check the fat content on the package. For an even lighter version, make the dish with maifun rice sticks, vermicelli noodles, or even soba.

Andy, one of my best friends, had a bunch of us over for dinner one night and made this amazing Mexican meatball soup. I went crazy for it—I mean who doesn't love a big bowl of soup filled with delicious turkey meatballs? What I love even more is that Andy says it's a "whatever you have in your kitchen" kind of thing. So feel free to add mushrooms, spinach, corn, or peppers. FWB: Ground turkey, avocado

Albóndigas (Meatball) Soup

SERVES 6

Meatballs

1 pound lean ground turkey

1/3 cup rice

1/4 cup finely chopped cilantro

1/4 cup finely chopped parsley

1/2 teaspoon ground cumin

1 1/2 teaspoons sea salt

1 large egg, lightly beaten

Soup

2 tablespoons extra-virgin olive oil

1 yellow onion, finely chopped

2 garlic cloves, finely minced

4 cups low-sodium chicken broth

2 tablespoons tomato paste

2 carrots, sliced 1/4 inch thick

1 large zucchini, cut into 1/4-inch half-moons

1 teaspoon dried oregano

3/4 teaspoon sea salt

1/2 teaspoon ground black pepper

1 avocado, sliced, for serving

1/2 cup finely chopped cilantro

1 lime, cut into wedges, for serving

To make the meatballs: Combine the ground turkey, uncooked rice, cilantro, parsley, cumin, and salt in a medium bowl. Use a wooden spoon to gently stir the mixture a couple of times to blend. Add the egg, mixing until everything is well combined. Pinch off large walnut-size bits of the mixture and roll them in your palms to make 1-inch balls. (You can cover the meatballs and refrigerate for a few hours if you like.)

To make the soup: Heat the oil over medium heat. Add the onion and cook, stirring occasionally, until soft, about 6 minutes. Stir in the garlic and cook until fragrant, about 1 minute. Add the chicken broth and 2 cups of water. Add the tomato paste and stir to combine. Once the tomato paste is dissolved, add the carrots and bring to a boil. Reduce the heat to medium-low and carefully add the meatballs, a few at a time. Cook the meatballs for 15 minutes, then add the zucchini. Continue to simmer the soup until the carrots and zucchini are tender and the meatballs are cooked through, 10 to 15 minutes longer. Stir in the oregano, salt, and pepper. Serve with avocado, if desired, a sprinkle of cilantro, and a lime wedge on the side for squeezing.

Per serving: 218 calories, 7 g fat (1 g saturated, 0 g trans), 23 g protein, 2 g fiber, 4 g sugars, 758 mg sodium, 17 g carbohydrates, 65 mg cholesterol

Ⓥ = vegetarian   Ⓥ = vegan

CHAPTER 4

Skinny-wiches & Wraps

If you've sworn off sandwiches because you think they aren't waist-friendly, then it's time to reassess the 'wich. With lean meat, veggies, and a good whole wheat wrap or bread, you have the fixings for something satisfyingly filling *and* healthy. The sandwiches in this chapter count on power carbs to keep you feeling good, like the complex kinds you get from multi-grain and whole wheat breads. Lean proteins like canned tuna, deli turkey, and hummus keep you going through the afternoon. These are a far cry from pre-packaged deli sandwiches that are loaded with fat, sodium, lots of calories from full-fat mayo, and empty carbs from white bread and rolls.

Grilling the vegetables after they've had a nice soak in a balsamic, lemon, and olive oil marinade gives these Balsamic Veggie Paninis (BVPs) a great smoky hit. The veggies can all be grilled at the same time—just don't overcrowd the grill pan or they'll steam instead of sear. I improvise a panini press using an extra skillet weighted down with a few cans of beans, but if you have a real panini press, by all means use it! FWB: Eggplant

Grilled BVPs

SERVES **4**

½ cup balsamic vinegar

4 tablespoons extra-virgin olive oil

2 tablespoons fresh lemon juice

I large eggplant, halved crosswise and sliced lengthwise into ⅛-inch-thick slabs

I large zucchini, halved crosswise and sliced lengthwise into ⅛-inch-thick slabs

I red bell pepper, thinly sliced

½ medium red onion, thinly sliced

8 thin slices sourdough or whole wheat bread (about ½ round loaf)

I teaspoon sea salt

♡ Frugal & Fab

Save your leftover roasted veggies from dinner and turn them into a panini for lunch!

Whisk the vinegar, 3 tablespoons of the olive oil, and the lemon juice in a large bowl. Add the eggplant, zucchini, bell pepper, and red onion and toss to coat. Cover with plastic wrap and refrigerate for at least 15 minutes and up to I hour.

Drizzle a little of the remaining I tablespoon olive oil over each slice of bread and then sprinkle with the salt.

Heat a ridged cast iron grill pan over high heat. Use tongs to remove the veggies from the marinade and pop them onto the pan, cooking until they get nice grill marks on both sides, 6 to 8 minutes total. You'll probably have to grill them in 2 to 3 batches so as not to overcrowd the pan. Turn off the heat and wipe off the pan (you'll use it again later).

Turn half the bread slices oil-side down. Divide the veggies among them and top with the remaining bread slices, oil-side up. Reheat the pan for I to 2 minutes, until hot. Place one or two sandwiches in the pan and place another large skillet on top. Weight the skillet down with a few cans of beans and grill until both sides are browned, 2 to 3 minutes per side. Slice in half diagonally and serve pronto. Repeat with the remaining sandwiches.

Per serving: 360 calories, 13 g fat (2 g saturated, 0 g trans), 9 g protein, 13 g fiber, 14 g sugars, 638 mg sodium, 55 g carbohydrates, 0 mg cholesterol

Now really, there's no need for mayonnaise or heavy dressing when you can count on great ingredients to pack in the flavor. Avocados, cucumbers, watercress, and soy sauce give this wrap richness, crispness, moisture, and a savory quality that no fat-filled, creamy, ranch-laden sammie could ever come close to. FWB: Avocado

Cali-Fresh Wrap

SERVES **4**

4 large wraps or flatbreads

1 cucumber, thinly sliced crosswise

1 Hass avocado, thinly sliced

1 bunch watercress, tough stems discarded, chopped crosswise into 1-inch segments

2 tablespoons reduced-sodium soy sauce

2 tablespoons fresh lemon juice

Lay the wraps on a cutting board. Divide the cucumbers among the wraps, arranging them in a row down the middle. Lay avocado slices over the cucumber and then top with the watercress. Sprinkle the soy sauce over the cress and follow with the lemon juice. Wrap it up nice and tight, slice in half diagonally, and serve.

Per serving: 181 calories, 6 g fat (1 g saturated, 0 g trans), 6 g protein, 3 g fiber, 2 g sugars, 487 mg sodium, 26 g carbohydrates, 0 mg cholesterol

The 300 Skinnywrap Club

All of these wrap ideas offer up a great value for your wallet and your waist, and not one of them cracks the 300-calorie mark, if you use a 10-inch low-calorie wrap.

♥ TDF Hummus (page 49), roasted red peppers, arugula, lemon juice

♥ ¼ cup canned water-packed albacore tuna, chopped Granny Smith apple, Dijon mustard, nonfat Greek yogurt

♥ Cooked egg whites, baby spinach, sliced mushrooms, red bell peppers

♥ Grilled or roasted veggies, 1 tablespoon Skinny Pesto (page 133)

♥ 3 thin avocado slices, baby spinach, roasted red peppers, dollop nonfat Greek yogurt

♥ Lean deli chicken (or leftover roast chicken), romaine lettuce, sliced Fuji apple, Dijon mustard

♥ 2 tablespoons chopped walnuts, baby spinach, sliced grapes, nonfat Greek yogurt

If you cut the cucumber sandwiches into quarters, they make a great snack or brunch hors d'oeuvre and can serve twice as many people. Don't forget to lift that pinky finger when you eat this skinnywich—it'll make you feel that much more fab! FWB: Whole wheat bread

Dill-Lite-Full Cucumber Tea 'Wiches

SERVES **4**

4 ounces $\frac{1}{3}$-less-fat Neufchâtel cream cheese, at room temperature

$\frac{1}{4}$ cup chopped fresh dill

2 teaspoons dried chives or 1 heaping tablespoon chopped fresh chives

$\frac{1}{2}$ teaspoon sea salt

8 slices whole wheat bread

1 cucumber

Mix the cream cheese, dill, chives, and sea salt together in a medium bowl until smooth. Spread 1 tablespoon on each slice of bread.

Cover half of the bread slices with cucumbers. Top with the remaining slices, cheese-side down. Use a serrated knife to trim off the crusts and cut each sandwich into 3 oblong fingers.

Per serving: 220 calories, 8.5 g fat (4.5 g saturated, 0 g trans), 11 g protein, 5 g fiber, 4 g sugars, 574 mg sodium, 26 g carbohydrates, 23 mg cholesterol

Slim Scoop!

Choose organically raised cukes whenever possible so you can skip the step of peeling. Most conventionally farmed cucumbers have a waxy coating to increase shelf life and must be well scrubbed or peeled before serving.

An open-face sandwich only requires one slice of bread while still offering up a healthy portion of the good stuff—in this case, the tuna salad topping. For this opened up sandwich I pile on protein-rich and dee-lish tuna salad made with black beans, sweet corn, and curry powder. Eat it out of hand or use a knife and fork for a more psychologically satisfying lunch! The tuna salad keeps in the fridge for a few days. FWB: Curry powder

Tuna Curry Salad on Toast

SERVES **4**

3 tablespoons Dijon mustard

2 tablespoons light mayonnaise

1 tablespoon curry powder

2 cans (5 ounces each) water-packed albacore tuna, drained

2 celery stalks with leaves

½ small sweet onion (like Maui or Vidalia), finely chopped

½ cup canned black beans, rinsed and drained

½ cup corn kernels—frozen (thawed) or canned (rinsed)

4 slices whole wheat bread, toasted and halved on a diagonal

Whisk the mustard, mayonnaise, and curry powder together in a medium bowl. Add the tuna and stir to combine.

Remove the leaves from the celery stalks and set them aside for later. Finely chop the celery stalks and add them to the tuna mixture. Mix in the onion, black beans, and corn. Pile the salad onto the toast, top with the reserved celery leaves, and serve.

Per serving: 252 calories, 6 g fat (1.3 g saturated, 0 g trans), 23 g protein, 5 g fiber, 4 g sugars, 863 mg sodium, 26 g carbohydrates, 32 mg cholesterol

♥ Frugal & Fab

Save those celery leaves! They're like free herbs—I use them when I don't have fresh parsley in the fridge.

♥ Slim Scoop!

If you're not a canned tuna lover, make this salad with leftover roasted or canned chicken. It's just as yummy. Sometimes I add dried cranberries for a sweet zing.

In this tasty lo-cal wrap (my favorite post-run snack), I combine the flavors of spicy tuna maki rolls, and leave out the starchy rice, subbing chickpeas instead. Wrapped up in tender lettuce leaves, this is both cheaper and more filling than Japanese takeout. FWB: Chickpeas

Spicy Tuna Lettuce Wraps

SERVES **4**

2 tablespoons light mayonnaise

1 tablespoon black bean chili paste (see Slim Scoop)

2 cans (5 ounces each) water-packed albacore tuna, drained

½ cup canned chickpeas, rinsed, drained, and coarsely chopped

1 shallot, finely chopped, or 2 tablespoons finely chopped scallions

1 tablespoon finely chopped cilantro

¼ teaspoon sea salt

1 tablespoon fresh lemon juice

½ head Bibb, red leaf, or romaine lettuce, leaves separated

Whisk the mayonnaise and chili paste together in a medium bowl. Add the tuna, chickpeas, shallot (or scallions), cilantro, and salt and stir to combine. Sprinkle with the lemon juice and stir. Divide the tuna among the lettuce leaves. Wrap the leaves around the filling burrito-style (fold the sides in and over the filling and then tuck the bottom up and roll the wrap to enclose) and serve.

Per serving: 143 calories, 5 g fat (1 g saturated, 0 g trans), 16 g protein, 2 g fiber, 1 g sugars, 501 mg sodium, 7 g carbohydrates, 28 mg cholesterol

✔ Slim Scoop!

My hands-down favorite chili paste is the old-school one from Lan Chi: black bean sauce with chiles. It's super intense and gives these wraps an instant flavor boost without a ton of extra calories.

This is such a classic. For breakfast, brunch, lunch, or late night, it's filling and delicious. To save money and for a great flavor, I make my own chive cream cheese using reduced-fat cream cheese, fresh dill, and chives (fresh are great if you have them but dried work fine, too). FWB: Salmon

Lox on Pumpernickel

SERVES **4**

4 ounces ⅓-less-fat Neufchâtel cream cheese, at room temperature

¼ cup chopped fresh dill

2 teaspoons dried chives or I heaping tablespoon chopped fresh chives

½ teaspoon sea salt

8 slices pumpernickel bread

12 thin slices smoked salmon

Mix the cream cheese, dill, chives, and salt together in a medium bowl until smooth. Spread I tablespoon on each slice of pumpernickel. Lay 3 slices of lox on 4 of the bread slices, and cover with the other 4 pieces. Halve the sandwiches on a diagonal and serve.

Per serving: 250 calories, 9 g fat (5 g saturated, 0 g trans), 16 g protein, 3 g fiber, I g sugars, 675 mg sodium, 26 g carbohydrates, 42 mg cholesterol

Slim Scoop!

Made with rye flour, pumpernickel is an excellent alternative to wheat bread. Try to find the heartier Euro versions rather than the Americanized ones that have added molasses and sugar.

My pesto, which is made with almonds instead of pine nuts and without Parm, is leaner than the traditional fat-loaded (but oh so good!) Genovese-style pesto. Because there is less fat, the flavors of the basil and lemon really shine. This wrap is substantial enough to keep you going all afternoon. Who says you can't have it all? FWB: Basil

Skinny Chicken Pesto Wrap

SERVES **4**

4 flour tortillas or wraps (10-inch diameter)

4 tablespoons Skinny Pesto (page 133)

½ pound thinly sliced lean deli chicken

1 small Roma tomato, thinly sliced

8 crisp romaine lettuce leaves

Place the tortillas on a work surface and spread each with 1 tablespoon of the pesto, leaving a 1-inch border around the edges. Divide the chicken and tomato among the wraps and then cover with lettuce. Fold in the ends and roll them up tightly, then halve diagonally.

Per serving: 225 calories, 10 g fat (2 g saturated, 0 g trans), 15 g protein, 2 g fiber, 2 g sugars, 765 mg sodium, 26 g carbohydrates, 25 mg cholesterol

♥ Frugal & Fab

In the wintertime, vine-ripe tomatoes get awfully pricey. If you have sun-dried tomatoes in your pantry, feel free to use them instead.

♥ Slim Scoop!

Make up a sandwich before you go to bed and then when you're ready to leave in the morning, all you have to do is grab it out of the fridge. Homemade lunches let you control the calories—brilliant!

Chicken-Apple Salad Skinnywich

SERVES **4**

8 whole black peppercorns

4 garlic cloves

2 bay leaves

2 sprigs fresh thyme

2 large chicken breasts halves (6–8 ounces each), trimmed of excess fat

1 tablespoon light mayonnaise

1 tablespoon Dijon mustard

$\frac{1}{2}$ small red onion, finely chopped

1 small Fuji apple, finely chopped

$\frac{1}{4}$ teaspoon sea salt

8 slices pumpernickel, whole-grain, or whole wheat bread, toasted

Bring a large skillet of water to a boil. Add the peppercorns, garlic, bay leaves, and thyme. Reduce the heat to a medium-low and add the chicken breasts. Slowly poach (you want a bare simmer—just the occasional bubble) until cooked through, about 20 minutes. Remove the chicken from the pan and when cool enough to handle, cut into $\frac{1}{2}$-inch cubes.

Stir the mayonnaise, mustard, onion, apple, and salt together in a large bowl. Add the chicken and toss to combine. Divide the salad among 4 slices of bread and top with the remaining bread. Slice on the diagonal and serve.

Per serving: 292 calories, 4 g fat (1 g saturated, 0 g trans), 25 g protein, 5 g fiber, 5 g sugars, 702 mg sodium, 37 g carbohydrates, 51 mg cholesterol

Surprise! Fuji apples are one of the secret ingredients I add to sandwiches for crunch and a little sweetness. The crisp apples combined with the creamy hummus and turkey really work this sandwich hard! If I have a quarter avocado around, I'll slice it up and add it for the good fats. FWB: Lean turkey

Turkey-Fuji Pita

SERVES **2**

2 tablespoons hummus, homemade (page 49) or store-bought

2 tablespoons nonfat plain Greek yogurt

2 whole wheat pitas, halved

1 Fuji apple, halved and thinly sliced

8 thin slices lean deli turkey

½ cup baby spinach

Mix the hummus and yogurt together in a small bowl and divide it among the pita halves. Dividing evenly, fill the pita halves with the apple, turkey, and spinach. Serve immediately or wrap up for lunch.

Per serving: 208 calories, 3 g fat (0 g saturated, 0 g trans), 15 g protein, 12 g fiber, 11 g sugars, 558 mg sodium, 40 g carbohydrates, 15 mg cholesterol

Slim Scoop!

Making your lunch sandwich with a pita pocket (about 100 calories apiece) instead of two slices of bread can save you around 100 calories a day!

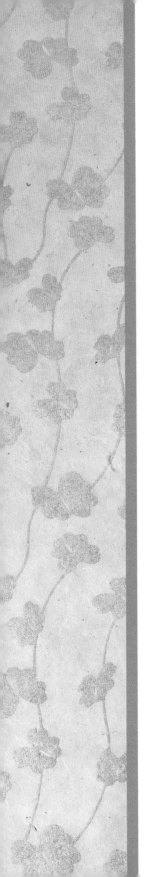

Ⓥ = vegetarian   ⓋⓃ = vegan

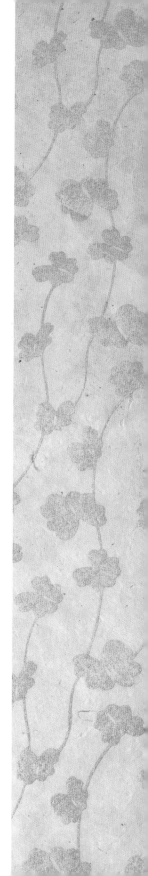

CHAPTER 5

Veggie Mains

Move over, meat! It's time you scootch to a less prominent position on the plate. You'll find 15 recipes here to show you how easy and delicious it can be. With a Japanese mom and a SoCal address, you can bet that I ate more than my share of tofu at home. Now that I'm all grown up, I am still crazy for tofu. It tastes clean and healthy and adds wonderful (cheap!) protein to salads and curries, marinara, sandwiches, whatever. In case you are not a tofu believer, there are also plenty of tofu-free veggie mains in this chapter, like my falafel (baked, not fried, thank you very much), two delicious pizzas, and even a svelte mac and cheese! You'll quickly find that tofu and veggie-inspired dishes are not only great on the waistline, but they will save you bundles of dinero, too.

For My Vegan Friends—Veganize It, Baby!

I would never leave my vegan friends out of the loop, especially when so many of my recipes are *nearly* vegan already. All you have to do is eliminate the tablespoon of Parmesan cheese or replace the honey with agave or maple syrup and there you have it. Here are great ways to veganize a recipe.

Instead of	Use
Butter	Oil (extra-virgin olive, canola, sesame) or all-natural buttery spread like Earth Balance
Buttermilk	Unsweetened almond milk or soymilk plus 2 teaspoons lemon juice
Chicken broth	Veggie broth
Chocolate chips	Vegan carob chips
Cream cheese	Tofutti Better Than Cream Cheese
Eggs (for cooking)	Crumbled extra-firm tofu
Eggs (for baking)	1 teaspoon baking soda plus 1 tablespoon apple cider or white vinegar or egg replacer, such as Ener G
Deli cheese	Soy- or nut-based vegan cheese slices
Deli meat	Thinly sliced savory baked tofu, sliced avocados, or grilled portobellos or grilled eggplant slices
Ground meat	Crumbled extra-firm tofu, crumbled tempeh, canned beans, or chopped portobello mushrooms
Honey	Agave syrup, maple syrup, or brown rice syrup
Mayonnaise	Vegan mayonnaise
Nonfat Greek yogurt	Coconut or soy yogurt
Nonfat milk	Unsweetened almond milk or soymilk
Parmesan	Chopped basil or chopped sun-dried tomatoes

Light and bright. That's how I feel after eating this beautiful composition of a dish. Quinoa, fresh basil, crunchy almonds, iron-rich spinach, and protein-packed tofu come together to create a super-good-for-you and great-tasting plate. It's smart, sexy, and so SoCal! To make this vegan, swap agave syrup for the honey. FWB: Quinoa

SoCal Quinoa and Cranberry Protein Plate

SERVES **6**

1½ cups quinoa

¾ cup coarsely chopped almonds or pistachios

2 cups chopped spinach

½ cup dried cranberries, finely chopped

¼ cup chopped fresh basil leaves

Half a 14-ounce package extra-firm tofu, cut into ½-inch cubes

¼ cup balsamic vinegar

1 tablespoon honey

¼ teaspoon sea salt

¼ teaspoon ground black pepper

2 tablespoons extra-virgin olive oil

♥ Slim Scoop!

Quinoa cooks up to be about the same shape as couscous and helps your body absorb nutrients, plus it's a complete protein. Why not make the swap?

Place the quinoa in a large bowl, cover with cold water, and then drain through a sieve. Place the quinoa in a medium saucepan with 3½ cups of water and bring to a boil over high heat. Reduce the heat to a simmer, cover, and cook until the quinoa is tender and has absorbed the liquid, about 25 minutes. Scrape the quinoa into a large bowl to cool.

Toast the nuts in a small dry skillet over medium heat until glossy and fragrant, 4 to 6 minutes, shaking the skillet occasionally. Transfer to a small plate and set aside.

Add the spinach, cranberries, and basil to the quinoa and toss to combine. Top with the tofu cubes. Whisk the balsamic vinegar with the honey, salt, and pepper. Whisk in the olive oil and pour the dressing over the salad, gently tossing to coat the leaves and tofu (trying not to break the tofu cubes). Cover the bowl with plastic wrap and refrigerate for at least 1 hour before serving. Transfer to a salad bowl or platter and sprinkle with the nuts before serving. It's delicious cold or at room temperature.

Per serving: 360 calories, 16 g fat (2 g saturated, 0 g trans), 13 g protein, 6 g fiber, 12 g sugars, 78 mg sodium, 44 g carbohydrates, 6 mg cholesterol

A little pan-sear and some love is all it takes to make this quick dish. It's a good one when you're slim on time but need to serve up something impressive. By keeping the rest of the ingredients lean, I can splurge on oh-my-goodness Gorgonzola! FWB: Onions

Pear and Onion Flatbreads with Gorgonzola and Walnuts

SERVES **6**

3 teaspoons extra-virgin olive oil

2 ripe but firm Bartlett or Bosc pears, halved and thinly sliced

1 medium yellow onion, halved and thinly sliced

4 lavash flatbreads or whole wheat pitas

$\frac{1}{2}$ teaspoon sea salt

$\frac{1}{2}$ cup coarsely chopped walnuts

$\frac{1}{2}$ cup crumbled Gorgonzola cheese

$\frac{1}{2}$ cup loosely packed fresh basil leaves, stacked, rolled, and thinly sliced crosswise

Heat 2 teaspoons of the olive oil in a large skillet over medium heat. Add the pears and onion and cook, stirring occasionally, until the pears are golden brown and juicy, 3 to 4 minutes. Turn off the heat and set the pan aside.

Heat a nonstick ridged cast iron grill pan over medium-high heat. Cook the flatbreads or pitas on both sides until they have grill marks. Transfer them to a platter and brush one side with the remaining 1 teaspoon olive oil and sprinkle with the salt. Top with the pear-onion mixture, walnuts, Gorgonzola, and basil. Cut into thirds and serve warm.

Per serving: 320 calories, 12 g fat (3 g saturated, 0 g trans), 9 g protein, 5 g fiber, 8 g sugars, 499 mg sodium, 45 g carbohydrates, 8 mg cholesterol

Slim Scoop!
This makes a gorgeous appetizer that takes no time at all to put together and tastes super luxe.

Pizza doesn't have to be a blob of grease, pools of cheese, and of questionable nutritional value. Instead I pile on the veggies and sub a hard grating cheese, like Parmesan, for the mozzarella. Parm packs in more robust flavor than mozzarella, so you can use less—and save calories. FWB: Artichokes, mushrooms

Grilled White Pizza with Mushrooms, Artichokes, and Parm

SERVES **4**

1 tablespoon plus 2 teaspoons extra-virgin olive oil

1 small red onion, halved and thinly sliced

6 garlic cloves, finely minced

1½ cups thinly sliced mushroom caps (any combination of white buttons, creminis, or portobellos)

1 can (15 ounces) artichoke hearts, drained and halved

½ teaspoon sea salt

All-purpose flour for rolling

1 pound store-bought pizza dough

3 tablespoons grated Parmesan cheese

6 basil leaves for serving

Heat 1 tablespoon of the olive oil in a large skillet over medium-high heat. Add the onion, reduce the heat to low, and cook, stirring occasionally, until the onions are deeply caramelized and sticky, about 20 minutes; if the onion starts to stick to the pan, splash the pan with a bit of water and stir to scrape up any browned bits.

Increase the heat to medium and stir in the garlic, cooking it until it is fragrant, 30 seconds to 1 minute. Stir in the mushrooms and cook until they just begin to soften and lose their moisture, 2 to 4 minutes. Stir in the artichoke hearts and ½ teaspoon of the salt and set aside.

Heat a grill to medium-high heat (or heat a ridged cast iron grill pan over medium-high heat). Sprinkle a work surface with flour and roll the dough into a round between ¼ and ½ inch thick. Brush the grill grates (or grill pan) with 1 teaspoon of the oil and gently lay the dough on the grates. Grill until the underside of the crust is golden, 1 to 2 minutes. Use a spatula to flip the dough over. Brush the remaining 1 teaspoon oil over the top of the dough and sprinkle with the remaining ½ teaspoon salt. Grill until the second side is golden, another 1 to 2 minutes. Transfer the grilled pizza round to a cutting board.

Top the pizza with the onion-artichoke mixture. Sprinkle with the Parmesan and finish with a few leaves of basil before slicing and serving.

Per serving: 370 calories, 12 g fat (1.5 g saturated, 0 g trans), 13 g protein, 4 g fiber, 4 g sugars, 1,000 mg sodium, 60 g carbohydrates, 3 mg cholesterol

Mushrooms, the Magical "Meaty" Veggie

If you're trying to limit your intake of animal protein but miss the robust, meaty flavor, then look no further than mushrooms. A great source of potassium and antioxidants, they're also super low in calories—just 18 per cup. Check out these great varieties:

Cremini: My favorite mushroom of all! These baby portobellos add richness and a great meaty texture to lasagna, pasta, or sautéed spinach with sun-dried tomatoes. Chop them, sauté them in olive oil with a pinch of sea salt, and add them to any recipe that needs a little bulking up.

White button: A little less flavorful than creminis, they can also be cheaper, too. I like to cook them whole and stuff them or use them raw in salads.

Portobello: Large, meaty, and juicy when cooked, versatile portobellos soak up any flavor you give them. They're super on a bun as a burger replacement and excellent chopped, sliced, sautéed, roasted, grilled, or breaded. Check out my portobello fries on page 196.

Shiitake: Nothing reminds me of my mom like the earthy flavor of fresh shiitakes sautéed in sesame oil with a dash of sea salt—they are TDF! Always remove the stem before cooking (it's very woody), but save them for making homemade veggie broth. To save cash, go for dried shiitakes instead.

Oyster: These delicately flavored 'shrooms add an exotic touch to pasta or a sautéed veggie dish. They have a slightly slippery texture when cooked, making them excellent in soups or saucy dishes.

Enoki (enokitake): These fragile and elegant Japanese mushrooms have long and pale white stalks that grow up to 4 inches long. They're lovely added to salads or used as a garnish for hot dishes like noodle soups or stir-fries.

While Mom is the queen of gyoza (see page 40), Dad's side of the family has a lock on pierogis, Polish dumplings. Compared to Grandma's pierogis, my take on them is a lot skinnier because I boil them instead of frying in butter. Served with a heap of sauerkraut, boiled pierogis make for a very satisfying meal. I like to make the filling and dough a day ahead and then invite a few friends over for a pierogi-making party. FWB: Mushrooms

Mushroom and Potato Pierogis

SERVES 6

Dough

1 cup all-purpose flour plus extra for kneading

1 teaspoon sea salt

2 large eggs, lightly beaten

2 tablespoons light sour cream

Filling

1 large russet (baking) potato (or 1 cup leftover mashed potatoes)

1 tablespoon extra-virgin olive oil

$\frac{1}{2}$ small yellow onion, finely chopped

$\frac{1}{2}$ cup finely chopped button mushroom caps

4 scallions, finely chopped

1 teaspoon sea salt

For serving

Sauerkraut

Nonfat plain Greek yogurt

To make the dough: Whisk the flour and salt together in a large bowl and make a well in the center of the mixture. Whisk the eggs, sour cream, and 2 tablespoons of water together and then pour it into the flour mixture. Gradually stir the flour into the egg mixture, slowly incorporating the flour until a dough begins to form (use a spoon at first and once the mixture becomes drier, it's best to mix with your hands).

Scrape the dough out onto a lightly floured work surface and knead, adding a sprinkle of flour occasionally to prevent sticking, until the dough is smooth and elastic, about 4 minutes. Cover the bowl with plastic wrap and let rest at room temperature for at least 15 minutes.

While the dough rests, make the filling: Place the potato in a medium pot of cold water and bring to a boil. Cook until a paring knife slips easily into the center, about 40 minutes. Drain, and once the potato is cool enough to handle, peel and mash it. Set aside. (Skip this step if using leftover mashed potatoes.)

Heat the oil in a medium nonstick skillet over medium heat. Add the onion and cook, stirring often, until soft and golden, about 5 minutes. Stir in the mushrooms and cook just until they release their liquid, 2 to 4 minutes. Add the mashed potatoes, scallions, and salt. Turn off the heat and set aside to cool to room temperature.

Dust a work surface with flour and divide the dough into quarters. Flour a rolling pin to keep the dough from sticking, and then roll one piece of dough into a large round that's no more than $\frac{1}{8}$ inch thick. Re-flour the work surface and rolling pin as needed to prevent sticking.

Set a small bowl of water next to your work area. Using a 3-inch round biscuit cutter (or the rim of a drinking glass), cut the dough into rounds. Place about 1 heaping teaspoon of filling in the center of each round. Dip your fingers in the water and moisten the edge of the round with water, then fold the other half over to make a half-moon shape. Press the edges together firmly to seal in the filling. Transfer the dumplings to a rimmed baking sheet dusted with flour and repeat with the remaining dough and filling. Cover the baking sheet with plastic wrap and chill the pierogi for 30 minutes or up to 2 hours (or freeze them in a single layer on a baking sheet and then transfer them to a resealable freezer bag for up to 6 months. The pierogis can be added to boiling water straight from the freezer.)

Bring a large pot of water to a boil. Salt the water then add about 10 dumplings (take care not to overcrowd the pot) and cook until the edges are tender, 8 to 10 minutes (they'll rise to the surface after 2 minutes). Remove them with a slotted spoon and place them in a large bowl. Cook the remaining dumplings and serve with plenty of sauerkraut and nonfat Greek yogurt.

Per serving (without toppings): 187 calories, 7.3 g fat (2.3 g saturated, 0 g trans), 6 g protein, 2 g fiber, 1 g sugars, 720 mg sodium, 24 g carbohydrates, 77 mg cholesterol

Slim Scoop!
I love to freeze my pierogis in reusable storage containers so that when I get that craving, I just thaw and nuke!

These are little pillows of herbed heaven in a bowl! When I'm in the mood to splurge, I'll finish these babies off with truffle oil and maybe a sprinkle of Parmesan. When I'm in the mood to scrimp, it's a simple drizzle of olive oil or even a spoonful of marinara that dresses them for dinner. Boil up what you need for a meal, and freeze the rest in a single layer on a rimmed baking sheet. Once frozen, slide them into a resealable freezer bag and store for up to 6 months.

Potato and Herb Gnocchi

SERVES **4**

2 large russet (baking) potatoes

1 large egg, lightly beaten

1½ cups all-purpose flour plus extra for shaping

¼ cup finely chopped fresh herbs (use whatever you have in the fridge; I like a combination of basil and oregano)

Sea salt

1 tablespoon extra-virgin olive oil

♥ Frugal & Fab

Don't let leftover roasted veggies go to waste. Mash them up and add them to the dough. My favorites are butternut squash, sweet potatoes, and even canned pumpkin (the plain stuff, not canned pumpkin pie filling).

Preheat the oven to 400°F. Use a fork to pierce the potatoes a few times and then wrap each one tightly in foil. Bake the potatoes until a paring knife slips easily into the center, about 1 hour. When the potatoes are cool enough to handle, peel, place them in a medium bowl, and mash with a fork.

Using a rubber spatula, mix in the egg and then sift in ¾ cup of the flour. Add the herbs and 1 tablespoon of salt and fold together. Sift in the remaining ¾ cup of flour and gently fold in until it is just combined. Take extra care not to overmix.

Liberally flour a work surface. Divide the dough into 6 equal pieces. With floured hands, roll each piece into a ¾-inch-thick rope, then cut the rope into ¾-inch segments. Transfer the gnocchi to a floured rimmed baking sheet and repeat with the remaining dough.

Bring a large pot of water to a boil. Add 1 teaspoon of salt and about 20 gnocchi. Boil until the gnocchi float to the surface, then cook until they are cooked through and tender, 3 to 4 minutes total. Use a slotted spoon to transfer the gnocchi to a large serving bowl. Drizzle with some of the oil and sprinkle with a little salt. Repeat with the remaining gnocchi, salt, and oil.

Per serving: 368 calories, 5 g fat (1 g saturated, 0 g trans), 10 g protein, 4 g fiber, 1 g sugars, 126 mg sodium, 70 g carbohydrates, 53 mg cholesterol

Curry is a comfort food that Mom used to make when I was growing up, and gathering around the table with my family for a big bowl of curried vegetables over rice is one of my warmest, fondest memories. The bold taste of curry powder is a great way to load up on flavor without adding extra fat or calories. FWB: Brown rice

3-Veg Curry over Brown Rice

SERVES 6

2 cups brown rice

1 tablespoon dark sesame oil

1 small yellow onion, finely chopped

3 tablespoons all-purpose flour

3 tablespoons curry powder

1½ cups warm vegetable broth

8 button mushroom caps, quartered

1 large carrot, finely chopped

1 celery stalk, finely chopped

1 cup canned chickpeas, rinsed and drained

1 large zucchini, finely chopped

1 tablespoon honey

½ teaspoon sea salt

Bring 4 cups of water to a boil in a large saucepan. Add the rice, stir once (no more!), return to a boil, reduce the heat to low, cover, and cook until the rice is tender, about 40 minutes. Cover and set aside until you're ready to serve.

While the rice cooks, make the curry sauce. Heat the sesame oil in a medium skillet over medium-high heat for 1 minute. Add the onion and reduce the heat to medium. Cook, stirring occasionally, until the onion is deeply caramelized and beginning to get sticky, 12 to 16 minutes; add 1 to 2 tablespoons of water if the onions start getting too brown or sticking to the pan. Stir in the flour and cook, stirring constantly, until it is golden, 4 to 6 minutes. Stir in the curry powder. Slowly whisk in some of the warm vegetable broth, starting with ¼ cup at a time, waiting until the consistency is smooth before adding the next addition. Once the mixture is loose and saucy, add all of the remaining broth and cook until the sauce is thick and creamy like an Alfredo sauce, about 5 minutes longer.

Add the mushrooms, carrot, celery, and chickpeas and cook for 15 minutes. Add the zucchini and continue cooking until all the vegetables are tender, about 5 minutes longer. Stir in the honey and salt and cook for 1 minute longer. Serve over the brown rice.

Per serving: 348 calories, 5.5 g fat (1 g saturated, 0 g trans), 10 g protein, 6 g fiber, 7 g sugars, 983 mg sodium, 67 g carbohydrates, 0 mg cholesterol

I can't imagine a Greek salad without lusciously briny olives. I chop them up extra fine and stir them into lemony tofu so you get olive flavor in every bite. The crumbled tofu replaces feta, and also helps to curb the olives' salty finish. Add some crunchy cukes and fresh herbs and you have a fabulously fit and flavorful meal. I love it with a few toasted pita triangles seasoned with a smidge of olive oil and a pinch of flaky salt. FWB: Olives

The Sleek Greek Center Plate Salad

SERVES 4

1 small red onion, finely chopped

1 cup pitted kalamata olives, finely minced

5 tablespoons fresh lemon juice (about 1½ lemons)

2 tablespoons extra-virgin olive oil

2 teaspoons dried oregano

1½ teaspoons sea salt

Ground black pepper

Half a 14-ounce package firm tofu, crumbled

2 plum tomatoes, finely diced

1 large cucumber, quartered lengthwise and sliced crosswise into small triangles

2 tablespoons finely chopped flat-leaf parsley

Whisk together the onion, olives, 4 tablespoons of the lemon juice, 1 tablespoon of the olive oil, the oregano, 1 teaspoon of the salt, and some pepper in a medium bowl. Add the tofu, stir to combine, cover the bowl with plastic wrap, and refrigerate for 30 minutes.

Toss together the tomatoes, cucumber, and parsley in a large bowl. Add the remaining 1 tablespoon lemon juice, 1 tablespoon olive oil, and ½ teaspoon salt. Stir to combine and let it sit at room temperature for 20 minutes.

Divide the tomato mixture among 4 plates. Sprinkle the tofu, onion, and olives over the tomatoes and cucumbers (leave any extra liquid in the bowl) and serve.

Per serving: 183 calories, 14 g fat (2 g saturated, 0 g trans), 5 g protein, 2 g fiber, 3 g sugars, 938 mg sodium, 11 g carbohydrates, 0 mg cholesterol

A veggie chili that is easy, hearty, and bursting with flavor? No way you say? I'm here to say yes way! Who'da thought you could be slim and sexy *and* eat your chili, too? For a vegan take, eliminate the Greek yogurt topping. This is a good one to serve up to people who think they don't like tofu! FWB: Tofu

Protein-Packed Veggie Chili

SERVES **6**

1 tablespoon canola oil

1 medium yellow onion, finely chopped

1 green or red bell pepper, finely chopped

1 package (14 ounces) firm tofu, crumbled

1 small jalapeño chile pepper, seeded, deribbed, and finely chopped (optional)

1 garlic clove, finely minced

2½ tablespoons chili powder

1 teaspoon ground cumin

1 bay leaf

1 teaspoon sea salt

½ teaspoon ground black pepper

1 can (28 ounces) diced tomatoes

1 can (15 ounces) black beans, rinsed and drained

1 can (15 ounces) kidney beans, rinsed and drained

6 tablespoons nonfat plain Greek yogurt (optional)

6 scallions, thinly sliced

Heat the oil in a large pot over medium-high heat. Add the onion and bell pepper, reduce the heat to medium, and cook, stirring occasionally, until very soft, about 10 minutes. Stir the tofu into the pot, then add the jalapeño (if desired), garlic, chili powder, cumin, bay leaf, salt, and black pepper. Cook, stirring often, until the garlic is fragrant, about 1 minute. Stir in the diced tomatoes (with juices), reduce the heat to low, cover, and cook, stirring occasionally, until it is thick, about 45 minutes.

Add the beans and cook until the beans are warmed through, 5 to 8 minutes. Taste and add more salt or pepper if needed. Serve topped with a dollop of yogurt, if desired, and a handful of scallions.

Per serving: 181 calories, 5 g fat (0.5 g saturated, 0 g trans), 11 g protein, 8 g fiber, 6 g sugars, 930 mg sodium, 25 g carbohydrates, 0 mg cholesterol

♥ Frugal & Fab

This "throw and go" recipe feeds a whole group for just a few bucks. If you're rollin' solo, freeze the leftovers in individual servings for lunch or dinner. Besides in a bowl, chili is great in burritos, as a chip dip, or even on slices of whole-grain bread for a healthy sloppy Joe.

I originally came up with this recipe as a way to use up some leftover quinoa, but the burgers are so tasty that I now make quinoa specifically for the burgers! They're so loaded with flavor that you'll never look at a veggie burger in the same way again. Meaty mushrooms are an excellent stand-in for beef. The bran gives the burger heft, and the soy sauce adds an earthy quality without making the burger taste "Asian." FWB: Quinoa

Quinoa-Mushroom Burgers

SERVES 4

1 cup raw quinoa or 2 cups cooked quinoa

1 cup finely chopped cremini or portobello mushroom caps

1/4 medium yellow onion, finely minced

1/2 cup panko bread crumbs or dried whole wheat bread crumbs

1/4 cup brown or Dijon mustard

2 tablespoons wheat bran

2 tablespoons reduced-sodium soy sauce

1 teaspoon extra-virgin olive oil

12 large Bibb lettuce leaves or 4 toasted whole wheat buns

1 tomato, thinly sliced

1 avocado, sliced

If starting with raw quinoa, place it in a large bowl, cover with cold water, and then drain through a sieve. Place it in a medium saucepan with 4 cups of water and bring to a boil over high heat. Reduce the heat to low and simmer, covered, until the quinoa is tender and has absorbed the liquid, about 25 minutes. Scrape the quinoa into a large bowl to cool.

Using a rubber spatula, mix the cooked quinoa, mushrooms, onion, bread crumbs, mustard, bran, and soy sauce. Shape the mixture into 4 1/2-inch-diameter patties.

Heat the olive oil in a medium nonstick skillet over medium-high heat. Add the patties and cook for 3 to 4 minutes on each side, or until crisp and golden. If serving with a Hollywood-style lettuce "bun," then slightly overlap 2 lettuce leaves on a plate, set the burger on the lettuce, and top with a tomato slice, an avocado slice, and another lettuce leaf. Serve immediately. (Or serve on whole wheat buns topped with tomato and avocado.)

Per serving: 246 calories, 9 g fat (1 g saturated, 0 g trans), 8 g protein, 7 g fiber, 2 g sugars, 473 mg sodium, 33 g carbohydrates, 0 mg cholesterol

On the weekends I regenerate. I rest my bod, my brain, and recharge with soulful food like these spicy soba noodles. I love eating these in bed with nothing else except for a *Sex in the City* rerun or *Women's Health* magazine to keep me company. FWB: Soba noodles, mushrooms

Spicy Soba with Shiitakes and Peas

SERVES **4**

2 tablespoons sesame seeds

1 tablespoon dark sesame oil

6 garlic cloves, finely minced

1 teaspoon grated fresh ginger

1 teaspoon red-pepper flakes

1 cup orange juice (preferably freshly squeezed)

2 tablespoons reduced-sodium soy sauce

¼ teaspoon sea salt, or to taste

1 package (8 to 10 ounces) soba noodles

1 cup frozen peas

1 cup fresh shiitake mushroom caps, thinly sliced, or ½ cup dried shiitake mushrooms soaked in hot water for 5 minutes, drained, and chopped

1 cup baby spinach or coarsely chopped large-leaf spinach

4 scallions, thinly sliced on the diagonal

Place the sesame seeds in a small skillet over medium heat and cook, shaking the pan often, until they get fragrant and toasty, 1 to 2 minutes. Pour them into a small bowl and set aside.

Heat the sesame oil in a large skillet over medium heat. Add the garlic, ginger, and red-pepper flakes and cook, stirring often, until the garlic is fragrant, about 30 seconds. Add the orange juice and soy sauce, increase the heat to high, and bring to a simmer. Reduce the heat to low and cook until the sauce is thick, syrupy, and reduced by half, about 20 minutes.

Meanwhile, bring a large pot of water to a boil. Add the salt and the soba noodles and cook for 5 minutes. Add the peas and boil until the peas are warmed through and the soba is cooked through, about 1 minute longer. Drain and set aside.

Stir the shiitakes into the orange sauce and increase the heat to medium. Cook, stirring occasionally, until the shiitakes are tender, 2 to 3 minutes. Stir the noodles and peas into the sauce and add the spinach. Toss everything together with tongs and continue to cook, tossing the pasta occasionally, until the spinach is wilted, about 2 minutes. Serve sprinkled with the sesame seeds and scallions.

Per serving: 383 calories, 7 g fat (1 g saturated, 0 g trans), 17 g protein, 5 g fiber, 8 g sugars, 912 mg sodium, 68 g carbohydrates, 0 mg cholesterol

Watch out—this baby cooks up quick! The best tactic is to have all of the veggie mix-ins and the sauce ready to go in small bowls near your cooktop. Prepping them all out ahead of time makes cooking homemade pad Thai a totally tasty breeze. If you like it spicy, add a squeeze of hot sauce or chili paste at the end for a kick. FWB: Tofu

Skinny Tofu Pad Thai

SERVES **4**

½ pound dried flat rice stick noodles

3 tablespoons tomato paste

3 tablespoons reduced-sodium soy sauce

2 tablespoons fresh lime juice

1 tablespoon honey

1 teaspoon ground ginger

1 large egg, lightly beaten (optional)

½ small yellow onion, very finely chopped

4 garlic cloves, finely minced

Half a 14-ounce package firm tofu, cut into 1-inch cubes

1 cup snow peas, trimmed and thinly sliced on the diagonal

1 cup bean sprouts

2 tablespoons dark sesame oil

¼ cup coarsely chopped cilantro (optional)

¼ cup Asian Almonds (page 55)

Sriracha (optional)

1 lime, cut into wedges

Place the noodles in a large bowl and cover with boiling water. Soak for 5 minutes, drain, and rinse under cold water. Set aside.

Whisk the tomato paste, soy sauce, lime juice, honey, and ginger in a small bowl. Place the following in separate bowls: the beaten egg (if desired); the onion and garlic; the tofu; the snow peas and and ½ cup of the bean sprouts; and ½ cup of water. Arrange them near your cooktop.

Heat 1 tablespoon of the sesame oil in a large skillet or wok over medium-high heat. Pour in the beaten egg and cook, stirring, until the egg is scrambled, about 1½ minutes. Scrape the egg into a bowl. Turn off the heat and wipe the skillet out with a damp paper towel. Use a wooden spoon to break the eggs up into small pieces and set aside.

Pour the remaining 1 tablespoon sesame oil into the clean skillet and heat over medium-high heat until the oil is just starting to smoke, 2 to 3 minutes. Add the onion and garlic and cook, stirring constantly, until just starting to turn golden, about 1 minute. Add the tofu and cook and stir gently until it is warmed through, 1 to 2 minutes. Stir in the tomato-soy mixture. Add the snow peas and bean sprouts. Cook for 1 minute, then add the water

(continued)

and drained noodles. Toss with tongs to combine. Cook, stirring often, until the noodles are cooked through and tender but still retain some springiness (use the package directions for timing guidelines).

Stir in the scrambled egg and cilantro, if desired, and turn off the heat. Top the pad Thai with the remaining $1/2$ cup bean sprouts. Serve with small bowls of Asian Almonds and sriracha, if desired, with lime wedges on the side.

Per serving: 365 calories, 9.4 g fat (1.3 g saturated, 0 g trans), 10 g protein, 5 g fiber, 9 g sugars, 447 mg sodium, 63 g carbohydrates, 0 mg cholesterol

When Fats Are Friendly

I think we all know we need to limit the amount of "bad fats" in our diet. This includes the saturated fat found in animal products (including cheese and milk) as well as trans fats (found in fried foods and solid shortening). But some fats are good for you—like the heart-healthy omega-3 fatty acids found in nuts and oily fish. (Omega-3s are a natural brain booster and beauty bonus for great skin and hair.) Other healthful fats are the monounsaturated fats that you get from olives, olive oil, and avocados.

If you use the "good fats" in place of "bad fats," you can actually reduce your risk of heart disease. Of course moderation is always key—too much of *any* fat is never cool. Just don't freak out from the fat you find in healthy whole ingredients like olives, avocados, nuts, and fish. Used in a smart way, fat can be a skinny asset!

If my dad, who is a total farm boy and cycles 15 miles a day, can dig into a plate of tofu like it's a slab of steak, then any man can! This marinara is loaded with texture and protein and turns already hearty whole wheat spaghetti into an even more filling meal. It's wonderful used in lasagna too, like the one on page 125. FWB: Tomatoes, tofu

Herbed Tofu Marinara with Whole Wheat Spaghetti

SERVES **6**

1 tablespoon extra-virgin olive oil

1 small yellow onion, finely chopped

2 garlic cloves, finely minced

Half a 14-ounce package firm tofu, crumbled

1 can (28 ounces) crushed tomatoes

1 teaspoon dried oregano

2 teaspoons sea salt

1 tablespoon balsamic vinegar

1 pound whole wheat spaghetti

4 teaspoons grated Parmesan cheese

Heat the olive oil in a large pot over high heat. Add the onion and cook until soft, stirring often, about 6 minutes. Add the garlic and cook until fragrant, about 30 seconds. Stir in the tofu. Add the tomatoes, oregano, and 1 teaspoon of the salt. Bring to a simmer, reduce the heat to medium-low, and cook until the sauce has reduced and thickened slightly, about 15 minutes. Stir in the vinegar and turn off the heat.

While the sauce cooks, bring a large pot of water to a boil. Add the remaining 1 teaspoon salt and the pasta. Cook until al dente, following the package instructions. Drain and toss with the sauce. Serve with a sprinkle of Parmesan.

Per serving: 369 calories, 5 g fat (1 g saturated, 0 g trans), 17 g protein, 12 g fiber, 8 g sugars, 744 mg sodium, 68 g carbohydrates, 1 mg cholesterol

Veggie lasagna is so delicious that you'll never miss all that greasy meat. Mushrooms and summer squash plus my tofu marinara (page 123) are the stars of this show and no-cook lasagna noodles make it super-easy. Get ready to convert your friends and family to the light side! FWB: Tofu, basil

Summer Squash and Mushroom Lasagna

SERVES 8

1 tablespoon extra-virgin olive oil

1 yellow onion, finely chopped

4 garlic cloves, finely minced

10 ounces button or cremini mushroom caps, thinly sliced

1 teaspoon sea salt

Herbed Tofu Marinara (page 123)

9 no-boil lasagna noodles

1 large yellow summer squash, halved lengthwise and thinly sliced crosswise

1 large zucchini, halved lengthwise and thinly sliced crosswise

¾ cup finely chopped fresh basil leaves

½ cup grated Parmesan cheese

Preheat the oven to 350°F.

Heat the olive oil in a large skillet over medium-high heat. Add the onion and cook until soft, stirring often, 4 to 5 minutes. Stir in the garlic and cook until fragrant, about 1 minute. Add the mushrooms and cook, stirring occasionally, until the mushrooms are tender, about 7 minutes. Stir in the salt and set aside.

Spread 1 cup of the marinara in a 9 × 13-inch baking dish and top with 3 uncooked noodles. Cover with half of the squash, half of the mushrooms, ¼ cup of the basil, and 2 tablespoons of the cheese. Ladle 1 cup of marinara on top and then cover with 3 more noodles. Layer with the remaining squash and mushrooms, ¼ cup of the basil, and 2 tablespoons of the cheese. Cover with 1 cup of the marinara, the remaining 3 noodles, and remaining 1 cup marinara.

Cover the baking dish with foil and bake until the noodles and squash are tender and the sauce bubbles around the edges, about 50 minutes. Remove the foil, sprinkle with the remaining ¼ cup cheese, and bake uncovered for an additional 10 minutes. Remove from the oven and let the lasagna rest for at least 20 minutes before slicing. Sprinkle each portion with some of the remaining basil.

Per serving: 223 calories, 7 g fat (1.5 g saturated, 0 g trans), 11 g protein, 4 g fiber, 8 g sugars, 723 mg sodium, 31 g carbohydrates, 4 mg cholesterol

Good-for-you mac and cheese? Yes, there *is* a God! I use lo-cal almond milk to add richness and light cream cheese for that trademark creamy quality. A little bit of Parm goes a long way too, while fresh basil brightens up the entire dish. Broiled until bubbling, this mac and cheese is just the thing for cozy nights at home. FWB: Almond milk

Platinum Skinny Mac and Cheese

SERVES 4

1½ teaspoons sea salt

3 cups large elbow macaroni

3 cups unsweetened almond milk

¼ cup ⅓-less-fat Neufchâtel cream cheese, at room temperature

2 tablespoons all-purpose flour

2 teaspoons garlic powder

3 tablespoons finely chopped fresh basil leaves

4 tablespoons grated Parmesan cheese

Bring a large pot of water to a boil. Add ½ teaspoon of the salt and the macaroni and cook until al dente, following the package instructions. Drain and set aside.

Whisk the almond milk with the cream cheese, flour, and garlic powder in a large saucepan (it's okay if it's a little lumpy at first, the cream cheese will melt into the sauce as it warms up). Bring to a simmer over medium-high heat, then reduce the heat to low and cook until the sauce is the consistency of a creamy Alfredo sauce, about 20 minutes. Turn off the heat.

Adjust an oven rack to the upper-middle position and heat the broiler to high. Stir the macaroni, 2 tablespoons of the basil, 2 tablespoons of the cheese, and the remaining 1 teaspoon salt into the sauce. Divide the mixture among four 8-ounce ramekins (or use an 8-inch square baking dish) and place them on a rimmed baking sheet. Sprinkle the remaining 2 tablespoons cheese over the tops. Broil until the tops are bubbling and browned, 4 to 6 minutes (check the broiler often as heat intensity varies!). Sprinkle with the remaining 1 tablespoon basil and serve.

Per serving: 396 calories, 6 g fat (2 g saturated, 0 g trans), 15 g protein, 4 g fiber, 9 g sugars, 700 mg sodium, 72 g carbohydrates, 7 mg cholesterol

Baking falafel rather than deep-frying them is a much healthier take that doesn't sacrifice a bit of flavor. I shape them into patties rather than balls—there's more surface area for the crunchy bits, and they bake up a little quicker. Of course the whole package is fab stuffed into a pita, too, but it's extra nice as a lean bread-free plate. If you like, you can serve the platter with lettuce leaves for wrapping! FWB: Parsley, chickpeas

Baked Falafel Plate with Dill Yogurt Dip and Cuke Salad

SERVES **4**

Falafel

1 can (15.5 ounces) chickpeas, rinsed and drained

1 small yellow onion, quartered

8 scallions, quartered

2 garlic cloves, coarsely chopped

½ cup coarsely chopped parsley

½ cup panko bread crumbs or dried whole wheat bread crumbs (plus extra if needed)

1 teaspoon cayenne

1 teaspoon ground coriander

1 teaspoon ground cumin

½ teaspoon sea salt

Salad

1 tomato, thinly sliced

1 large cucumber, thinly sliced

½ small yellow onion, finely minced

2 tablespoons finely chopped parsley

1 tablespoon fresh lemon juice

½ teaspoon sea salt

Preheat the oven to 350°F. Line a rimmed baking sheet with foil and coat with cooking spray.

To make the falafel: Combine the chickpeas, onion, scallions, garlic, parsley, panko, cayenne, coriander, cumin, and salt in a food processor. Pulse to combine, then process until finely ground and the mixture holds together, 30 to 40 seconds. If the mixture doesn't hold together when you squeeze a pinch in your hand, then pulse in more breadcrumbs, 1 tablespoon at a time, until it does.

Pack a ¼-cup measuring cup with some of the mixture. Turn it out onto a work surface and press down using firm but light pressure to flatten it into a 3-inch patty. Place the patty on the baking sheet and repeat with the remaining falafel mixture to make 7 more patties. Bake until crisp and golden brown, 20 to 25 minutes. Set aside to cool slightly.

To make the salad: Toss the tomato and cucumber together in a medium bowl. Add the onion, parsley, lemon juice, and salt and toss to combine. Set aside at room temperature until you're ready to serve.

Dill yogurt dip

½ cup nonfat plain Greek yogurt
1 tablespoon finely chopped fresh dill
2 teaspoons fresh lemon juice

TDF Hummus (page 49), optional
Tender lettuce leaves

To make the dip: Stir the yogurt, dill, and lemon juice together.

To serve, divide the falafel and salad among 4 plates. Serve with the yogurt dip, and, if desired, hummus and lettuce leaves on the side.

Per serving: 169 calories, 1 g fat (0 g saturated, 0 g trans), 10 g protein, 6 g fiber, 6 g sugars, 66 mg sodium, 30 g carbohydrates, 0 mg cholesterol

Slim Scoop!

Make a big batch of falafel and freeze them. They are wonderful snacks for an on-the-go day or for a party. Just reheat in a warm oven or in a toaster oven. The dill dip is excellent with raw veggies, too—make a triple batch and keep it in the fridge (it's great for up to 1 week) for snacking.

Ⓥ = vegetarian　Ⓥ = vegan

CHAPTER 6

Fins & Shells

Growing up with an über-healthy Japanese mom, fish and shellfish have always been a major part of my diet—from grilled fish tacos beachside to Mom's miso salmon. I am definitely a huge seafood fanatic and try to eat it at least three times a week. Eating fish instead of other animal proteins boosts your omega-3 supply, which may protect your brain and heart, and also lowers the amount of saturated fat that you take in. Omegas-3s also may keep your hair and skin gorgeous. Eating fish should really be considered part of an ultimate beauty regime. Cheers to that!

Next to marinara, pesto is probably my favorite pasta sauce, but do you have any idea how much fat there is in that sauce loaded with cheese, pine nuts, and olive oil? It's a shocker. My skinny pesto is made with almonds (less fat than pine nuts) and no cheese. The flavor is fresh and fabulous—a true green goddess of a sauce! FWB: Almonds

Pan-Seared Scallops with Skinny Pesto Fettuccine

SERVES 6

Skinny Pesto

3 cups fresh basil leaves

$\frac{1}{2}$ cup raw almonds

1 garlic clove, coarsely chopped

$\frac{3}{4}$ teaspoon sea salt

$\frac{1}{2}$ cup extra-virgin olive oil

2 tablespoons fresh lemon juice

Scallops

$\frac{1}{4}$ cup plus 2 tablespoons fresh lemon juice (1–2 lemons)

2 tablespoons plus 2 teaspoons extra-virgin olive oil

$\frac{1}{2}$ teaspoon sea salt

18 large sea scallops, rinsed

1 pound whole wheat fettuccine

$\frac{1}{2}$ cup dry white wine

To make the pesto: Combine the basil, almonds, garlic, and salt in a food processor and pulse until somewhat mealy. Gradually add the olive oil, processing until the mixture is finely chopped yet still has texture, about 1 minute. Pulse in the lemon juice.

To prepare the scallops: Whisk together $\frac{1}{4}$ cup of the lemon juice, 2 tablespoons of the olive oil, and $\frac{1}{2}$ teaspoon of the salt in a medium bowl. Add the scallops, turn to coat, cover with plastic, and refrigerate for 10 minutes.

Meanwhile, bring a large pot of salted water to a boil. Add the pasta and cook until al dente, according to the package instructions. Drain well.

Heat the remaining 2 teaspoons olive oil in a large skillet over medium heat. Add the scallops and cook, without turning, until nicely browned on the bottom, about 3 minutes. Turn and cook the other side until browned, another 2 to 3 minutes. Set aside on a plate.

Add the wine and remaining 2 tablespoons lemon juice to the skillet. Scrape up any browned bits and simmer until the sauce is reduced by half, 1 to 2 minutes. Add the fettuccine to the skillet along with the pesto. Turn off the heat and toss everything together. Arrange 3 scallops on a plate and serve hot.

Per serving: 558 calories, 27 g fat (3 g saturated, 0 g trans), 23 g protein, 10 g fiber, 1 g sugars, 485 mg sodium, 52 g carbohydrates, 15 mg cholesterol

This dish is so quick to whip up it will make your head spin! Bok choy is an incredible vegetable. Its white stalks have a wonderful fresh flavor, and the green tops are incredibly mild and tender. Best of all, it's often hiding out in your produce section for $1 to $2 per pound—what a score! This recipe calls for fresh Chinese egg noodles—if you can't find them, you can use whole wheat angel hair pasta instead. FWB: Bok choy

Lemony Shrimp and Bok Choy Lo Mein

SERVES 4

1 tablespoon sesame seeds

Sea salt

2 cups fresh Chinese egg noodles or dried angel hair pasta

1 tablespoon canola oil

2 garlic cloves, finely minced

1 head bok choy, stems sliced ½ inch thick on the diagonal and leaves coarsely chopped

½-inch piece fresh ginger, grated

2½ tablespoons reduced-sodium soy sauce

1 pound medium shrimp, peeled and deveined

1 teaspoon dark sesame oil

2 teaspoons fresh lemon juice

2 scallions, thinly sliced on the diagonal

Place the sesame seeds in a small skillet and heat over medium heat shaking the pan often, until fragrant and toasty, 1 to 2 minutes. Transfer to a small plate and set aside.

Bring a large pot of salted water to a boil. Add the noodles and boil until they are tender, 3 to 4 minutes. (If using dried pasta you may need to adjust the cooking time according to package instructions.) Drain and set aside.

Heat the canola oil in a large nonstick skillet over medium heat. Add the garlic and cook, stirring often, until fragrant, about 1 minute. Stir in the bok choy stems. Add the ginger and soy sauce and cook until the stems are just tender, about 3 minutes. Add the shrimp and cook, stirring often, until the shrimp begin to turn opaque, about 2 minutes. Stir in the drained noodles and toss to coat. Stir in the bok choy greens and sesame oil and cook, tossing often, until they just begin to wilt, about 4 minutes. Finish with the lemon juice, sesame seeds, and scallions. Serve hot.

Per serving: 320 calories, 8 g fat (1 g saturated, 0 g trans), 37 g protein, 3 g fiber, 3 g sugars, 964 mg sodium, 30 g carbohydrates, 177 mg cholesterol

Store-bought wonton wrappers let you make homemade raviolis without the hassle of kneading and rolling pasta dough. Stuff them with sweet canned crabmeat and plump shiitakes—you can't go wrong. Uncooked raviolis freeze beautifully, so you may want to make a double batch, or serve half now, half later. FWB: Mushrooms, spinach

Crab and Mushroom Ravs

SERVES **6**

1 tablespoon extra-virgin olive oil

8 ounces cremini, shiitake, or oyster mushrooms, stems discarded and caps finely chopped

4 garlic cloves, finely minced

5 ounces (about 4 cups) baby spinach, chopped

Sea salt

$^3/_4$ cup part-skim ricotta cheese

4–6 ounces crabmeat, fresh or canned

$^1/_4$ cup unsalted dry-packed sun-dried tomatoes, finely chopped (if they're really hard, soak in warm water for 10 minutes and drain before chopping)

1 package (12 ounces) round wonton wrappers

2 cups store-bought marinara sauce or Herbed Tofu Marinara (page 123)

2 tablespoons grated Parmesan cheese

$^1/_4$ cup torn, whole, or shredded basil leaves

Heat the olive oil in a large skillet over medium-high heat. Add the mushrooms and cook, stirring occasionally, until they begin to brown, about 4 minutes. Add the garlic and cook, stirring, until it is fragrant, about 1 minute. Stir in the spinach and $^1/_2$ teaspoon of salt and cook, stirring often, until the spinach is wilted, about 1 minute. Turn off the heat and let the mixture cool slightly. Stir in the ricotta, crabmeat, and sun-dried tomatoes.

Place a small bowl of water next to your work surface. Cover the wonton wrappers with a damp paper towel to keep them from drying out. Working with 2 wonton wrappers at a time, place about 1 tablespoon of the filling in the center of one. Use your finger to wet the exposed part (not just the edges) of the wrapper with water. Cover with the second wrapper, pressing together to seal. Repeat with the remaining wrappers and filling.

Bring a large pot of salted water to a boil. Add about half of the raviolis, stir gently, and return to a gentle simmer. Once they float to the surface, cook for 3 to 4 minutes. Remove them using a frying spider or slotted spoon, place them on a plate, and set aside. Repeat with the remaining raviolis. Serve topped with the marinara sauce, Parmesan, and basil.

Per serving: 323 calories, 7 g fat (2.4 g saturated, 0 g trans), 17 g protein, 5 g fiber, 4 g sugars, 998 mg sodium, 47 g carbohydrates, 31 mg cholesterol

I don't know who gets invited to more parties—me or my crab cakes! While cooking on the line at high-end restaurants and resorts, I learned that panko bread crumbs are the key to stretching out a pound of crabmeat to feed six people! Everyone always thinks that crab cakes are so difficult to prepare, but in reality they're easy—just stir together, form, and brown. FWB: Red bell pepper

Fresh Fuji Crab Cakes

SERVES **6**

Crab cakes

16 ounces lump crabmeat, fresh or canned

1 small red onion, finely chopped

½ red bell pepper, finely chopped

2 tablespoons finely chopped cilantro

Juice of 1 lemon

1 tablespoon reduced-sodium soy sauce

2 teaspoons dark sesame oil

1 Fuji apple, cut into thin matchsticks

3 tablespoons light mayonnaise

1 large egg, lightly beaten

2 cups panko bread crumbs

2 tablespoons canola oil

To make the crab cakes: Stir the crabmeat, onion, bell pepper, cilantro, lemon juice, soy sauce, and sesame oil together in a medium bowl. Stir in the apple. Add the mayonnaise, mixing until all of the ingredients are evenly coated. Add the egg and stir to combine. Stir in 1 cup of the panko. Use your hands to pack the mixture tightly into twelve 2-inch-diameter patties, 1 inch thick.

Place the remaining 1 cup of panko in a shallow dish. Coat the patties with panko and place them on a baking sheet.

Heat 1 tablespoon of the oil in a large nonstick skillet over medium heat. Working in batches, add enough patties to fill the pan without crowding and cook, without turning, until golden brown, 2 to 3 minutes. Use a thin metal spatula to gently flip the crab cakes and brown the other side, an additional 2 to 3 minutes. Transfer to a paper towel–lined plate to drain. Repeat with the remaining crab cakes, adding half of the remaining 1 tablespoon oil to the pan for each batch.

Per (2-cake) serving: 332 calories, 16 g fat (2 g saturated, 0 g trans), 22 g protein, 2 g fiber, 6 g sugars, 579 mg sodium, 23 g carbohydrates, 118 mg cholesterol

Stuffed with fluffy quinoa, sweet crabmeat, fresh basil, and fragrant saffron, this all-in-one meal is a far cry from bland, heavy, rice-loaded peppers. Crab can be pricey when it's not on sale, so feel free to use chopped raw shrimp or shredded rotisserie chicken instead. FWB: Red bell pepper, quinoa

Quinoa and Crab-Stuffed Red Peppers

SERVES **6**

1 cup quinoa

1½ tablespoons extra-virgin olive oil

1 small yellow onion, finely chopped

8 ounces lump crabmeat

1 cup tomato sauce

¼ cup fresh basil leaves, stacked, rolled, and sliced crosswise into thin strips

Pinch of saffron

1 teaspoon sea salt

3 red bell peppers, halved lengthwise

✔ Slim Scoop!

Quinoa is gluten-free, making it a great option for people who can't tolerate wheat. It's also inexpensive and has more than 8 grams of protein per cup!

Place the quinoa in a large bowl, cover with cold water, and then drain through a sieve. Bring 2 cups of water to a boil in a medium saucepan and add the quinoa. Reduce the heat to low and simmer, covered, until the quinoa is tender and has absorbed the liquid, about 25 minutes. Scrape the quinoa into a large bowl to cool slightly.

Preheat the oven to 375°F.

Heat 1 tablespoon of the olive oil in a medium skillet over medium-low heat. Add the onion and cook until soft and golden, about 4 minutes. Stir in the crabmeat and tomato sauce and cook until warmed through, about 2 minutes. Remove from the heat and stir in the cooked quinoa, basil, saffron, and ½ teaspoon of the salt. Set aside.

Coat the insides of the pepper halves with the remaining 1½ teaspoons oil and arrange in a baking dish. Season with the remaining ½ teaspoon salt. Roast until just tender, about 25 minutes.

Remove the pan from the oven and place on a heatproof work surface. Mound ½ cup of the quinoa mixture in each pepper half and return to the oven until the peppers are soft and fragrant and the quinoa mixture is hot, about 15 minutes. Serve hot.

Per serving: 213 calories, 6 g fat (1 g saturated, 0 g trans), 14 g protein, 4 g fiber, 5 g sugars, 623 mg sodium, 25 g carbohydrates, 40 mg cholesterol

Paella is total party food: It feeds a crowd, it tastes exotic, and it is gorgeous on the table. This recipe is a keeper because it's delicious without a hint of fussy. I keep a lid on the cost by using budget-friendly mussels and shrimp. Make this one for your pals—trust me, they'll love you even more. FWB: Artichokes, brown rice

One-Pan Paella

SERVES **8**

2 tablespoons extra-virgin olive oil

1 large yellow onion, coarsely chopped

1 tablespoon sea salt

3 garlic cloves, finely minced

1 cup cremini or button mushrooms, stemmed and coarsely chopped

2 cups brown rice

2 tablespoons tomato paste

2 pinches of saffron

1/2 cup dry white wine (optional)

4 cups low-sodium chicken broth

1 1/2 pounds large shrimp, peeled and deveined

1 pound cultivated mussels or littleneck clams, scrubbed under cold water

1 can (14 ounces) artichoke hearts, drained, rinsed, and quartered

1 lemon, halved

2 teaspoons hot paprika or red-pepper flakes

1 tablespoon finely chopped fresh basil or flat-leaf parsley leaves

Heat the olive oil in a large skillet over medium heat. Reduce the heat to medium-low, add the onion and salt, and cook, stirring occasionally, until the onions are lightly golden and soft, 13 to 15 minutes. Stir in the garlic and cook until fragrant, about 30 seconds. Add the mushrooms and cook until they've released their liquid and are tender, about 5 minutes.

Add the rice, tomato paste, and saffron and cook, stirring, for 2 minutes, or until the rice is somewhat opaque. Stir in the wine, if desired. Add 3 1/2 cups of the chicken broth, increase the heat to medium-high, and bring to a boil. Reduce the heat to low, cover, and gently cook until the rice is just tender, 40 to 45 minutes.

Place the shrimp, mussels or clams, and artichokes on top of the rice. Pour in the remaining 1/2 cup broth, cover, and cook until the shrimp have cooked through and the mussels or clams have opened, 6 to 8 minutes (discard any that haven't opened).

Squeeze one lemon half over the paella and sprinkle with the paprika and basil or parsley. Slice the remaining lemon half into 4 wedges, then slice the wedges in half crosswise. Divide the paella among 8 bowls and serve with a lemon piece on the side.

Per serving: 387 calories, 7.7 g fat (1.3 g saturated, 0 g trans), 32 g protein, 3 g fiber, 2 g sugars, 974 mg sodium, 46 g carbohydrates, 149 mg cholesterol

Cream-based sauces are so last century—miso is where it's at. It tastes creamy and rich (see opposite page for more info on miso) and can boost the flavor of soups, salad dressings, sauces, and marinades without adding calories and fat. FWB: Salmon

Miso Gorgeous Glazed Salmon

SERVES 4

2 tablespoons red miso paste

2 tablespoons red wine vinegar

1 tablespoon honey

1½ teaspoons dark sesame oil

½ teaspoon reduced-sodium soy sauce

4 salmon fillets (6 ounces each), 1 inch thick

1 tablespoon black sesame seeds (optional)

2 scallions, thinly sliced on the diagonal

Preheat the oven to 350°F. Whisk the miso with the vinegar, honey, sesame oil, soy sauce, and 1 tablespoon of water to make a smooth paste.

Coat a 9 × 13-inch baking dish with cooking spray. Place the salmon fillets skin-side down in the pan and brush with about half of the marinade. Set aside for 10 minutes (or refrigerate for up to 1 hour) to marinate.

Brush the salmon with the rest of the marinade and bake until the salmon is opaque at the edges and still pink in the very center, about 20 minutes. Let cool for 5 minutes before serving, sprinkle with the sesame seeds (if desired) and scallions.

Per serving: 360 calories, 20 g fat (4 g saturated, 0 g trans), 34 g protein, 2 g fiber, 6 g sugars, 441 mg sodium, 8 g carbohydrates, 100 mg cholesterol

♥Frugal & Fab

Frozen salmon fillets are a great value. I buy a bag of seven for $20—that's less than $3 a fillet for a protein-packed, brain-boosting meal. Try to buy wild-caught rather than farmed if you can find it.

So Many Miso!

Miso is a best friend to soups, marinades, dressings, and glazes, and I love it for its health benefits too—like 2 grams of protein in every tablespoon plus trace minerals like manganese and zinc. The three most common types of this fermented soybean paste are red, white, and yellow. Here's a bit of info on all three:

White miso: This is the sweetest, smoothest miso of the three. It is made with a larger ratio of white rice to soybeans and has more carbs than red or yellow miso. It's nice when you want a more delicate miso flavor.

Yellow miso: With a little more pow than white miso, yellow miso adds more flavor but not as much pungency as red miso. It's most often made from soybeans fermented with barley and a smaller amount of rice. I like it for glazes and marinades.

Red miso: My favorite. Red miso has higher protein than white miso. It's made from grains, soybeans, and/or barley and gets fermented for longer (sometimes up to 3 years) than white or yellow miso. It has the most intense flavor and a gorgeous deep reddish color. A little dab will do ya.

My parents eat salmon at least once a week, and let me tell you, it shows! At nearly 60 years old, they're both brilliant, beautiful, and happy. Knowing how much they love salmon, I made this dish for their Valentine's date-night. The twist is an extra omega boost from the flaxseed rub. Check health food stores for flaxseed meal, and if you can't find it, give whole flaxseeds a whirl in your cleaned-out coffee grinder or in a food processor. FWB: Flaxseeds

Mega Omega Salmon

SERVES **4**

½ cup flaxseed meal

1 tablespoon dried basil

1 teaspoon garlic powder

½ teaspoon cayenne

1 lemon, halved

4 salmon fillets (8 ounces each)

½ teaspoon sea salt

Preheat the oven to 350°F. Lightly coat a 9 × 13-inch baking dish with cooking spray.

Stir the flaxseed meal, basil, garlic powder, and cayenne together in a medium bowl. Squeeze a lemon half (save the other half for serving) over the salmon, then season with the salt. Press the salmon fillets into the flaxseed mixture, coating both sides. Place the salmon skin-side down in the baking dish.

Bake the fillets until they yield only slightly to semifirm pressure and they flake easily, 18 to 20 minutes. Squeeze the remaining lemon half over the salmon and serve.

Per serving: 510 calories, 31 g fat (5 g saturated, 0 g trans), 48 g protein, 4 g fiber, 0.5 g sugars, 331 mg sodium, 6 g carbohydrates, 134 mg cholesterol

♥Frugal & Fab

Grab a couple of friends and buy a whole side of salmon (often less than buying it precut in fillets) and divvy it up at home—everyone gets to share the goodness and the savings!

Who knew that canned salmon was so tasty and easy to work with? Even though it's a lot cheaper than fresh salmon, you don't sacrifice any of the heart-healthy omega-3s. It's great in salads and sandwiches, but I especially love canned salmon in these crispy salmon burgers loaded with peppers, corn, and chiles. The chive-yogurt sauce is just the thing to tame the heat! FWB: Salmon

Spicy Salmon Burgers with Creamy Chive Sauce

SERVES **6**

Burgers

2 tablespoons light mayonnaise

2 tablespoons fresh lime juice

1 large egg

1 tablespoon reduced-sodium soy sauce

$^1\!/_2$ teaspoon cayenne

$^1\!/_2$ teaspoon sea salt

$^1\!/_2$ red bell pepper, finely chopped

$^1\!/_2$ small red onion, finely chopped

$^1\!/_2$ cup corn kernels, frozen (thawed) or canned (rinsed)

1–2 tablespoons minced canned green chiles or chipotles

$1^1\!/_4$ cups panko bread crumbs

3 cans (5 ounces each) boneless and skinless salmon, drained

2 tablespoons canola or vegetable oil

Sauce

$^1\!/_2$ cup nonfat plain Greek yogurt

$^1\!/_4$ cup finely chopped chives

1 teaspoon Worcestershire sauce

To make the burgers: Whisk the mayonnaise, lime juice, egg, and soy sauce together in a medium bowl. Whisk in the cayenne and salt. Add the bell pepper, onion, corn, and chiles. Once they're well combined, stir in the panko. Gently stir in the salmon.

Divide the mixture into 6 equal parts and shape each into a ball, then pat into 3-inch-diameter patties, 1 inch thick.

Heat a medium regular or cast iron skillet over medium-high heat. Add the oil, reduce the heat to medium, and add the patties. Cook until they're golden brown on the bottom, 2 to 3 minutes. Use a spatula to gently turn them over and brown the other side for an additional 2 to 3 minutes. Transfer them to a paper towel–lined plate.

To make the sauce: Whisk the yogurt, chives, and Worcestershire sauce together in a small bowl.

Serve the burgers with a dollop of the sauce.

Per serving: 224 calories, 11 g fat (1.5 g saturated, 0 g trans), 18 g protein, 1 g fiber, 3 g sugars, 566 mg sodium, 15 g carbohydrates, 83 mg cholesterol

Easy, delicious, and gorgeous. I make this recipe whenever I need a taste of summertime. Mahi-mahi is a wonderfully steak-y fish. If you can't find it, you could use striped bass, salmon, or Arctic char instead. The black bean salsa is super versatile—it's great with grilled chicken, shrimp, and scallops. FWB: Avocado

Pan-Seared Mahi-Mahi with Black Bean Salsa

SERVES 4

4 tablespoons lime juice (2 or 3 limes)

1 tablespoon plus 1 teaspoon extra-virgin olive oil

1 teaspoon sea salt

2 cups corn kernels, fresh or frozen

1 cup canned black beans, rinsed and drained

1 small red onion, finely chopped

1/4 cup finely chopped roasted red peppers (see opposite)

3 tablespoons finely chopped cilantro

4 mahi-mahi fillets (4–6 ounces each)

1 semiripe Hass avocado, cut into 1/2-inch cubes

Whisk 3 tablespoons of the lime juice, 1 tablespoon of the olive oil, and 1/2 teaspoon of the salt together in a large bowl. Stir in the corn, beans, onion, roasted peppers, and cilantro. Cover with plastic wrap and refrigerate until serving (the salsa can be made up to 12 hours in advance).

Place the fish fillets on a work surface and sprinkle with the remaining 1 tablespoon lime juice and remaining 1/2 teaspoon salt. Heat the remaining 1 teaspoon olive oil in a large nonstick skillet over medium-high heat. Add the fish skin-side down and cook until golden brown, 4 to 6 minutes. Use a thin metal spatula to flip the fillets and cook on the other side until golden brown, another 4 to 6 minutes. Remove from the heat and set aside.

Add the avocado to the salsa and gently stir to combine. Place one fillet on each plate and top with some salsa. Serve hot.

Per serving: 284 calories, 7 g fat (1 g saturated, 0 g trans), 28 g protein, 8 g fiber, 5 g sugars, 771 mg sodium, 31 g carbohydrates, 83 mg cholesterol

4 Steps to Homemade Roasted Peppers

Roasted red peppers are a cinch to make at home, and if you make them when peppers are in season and cheap, it will save you bundles of dinero since you don't have to pay the premium for jarred or deli-packed peppers.

1. Using tongs, hold a red bell pepper over an open flame. Roast it, turning often, until all sides are charred and blackened. (If you don't have gas burners, you can broil them instead; place the peppers on a rimmed baking sheet on the upper-middle rack of your oven and turn the pepper often to char it on all sides.)

2. Place the pepper on a square of plastic wrap and tightly wrap up. Set aside for 5 minutes.

3. Unwrap the peppers and peel away the skin using a wet paper towel to help you remove all the charred bits.

4. Pull out the stem and use a paring knife to scrape away the ribs and seeds. Refrigerate the peppers for up to 5 days. If you want to keep them longer, place them in a jar and cover with a neutral flavored oil, such as canola or grapeseed.

My many surfing trips to Mexico have all had one thing in common (well, besides surfing!): super-yummy fish tacos. On a hot summer day and with an icy-cold 'rita on the side, there's nothing more satisfying. Grill them on the barbie if the weather allows; if not, use a grill pan, it'll be just fine. With a squeeze of lime and some tequila-lime sauce, you're all smiles, baby! FWB: Cabbage, fish

Fabulous Fish Tacos with Tequila-Lime Sauce and Pickled Slaw

SERVES 6

Slaw

³/₄ cup sugar

³/₄ cup apple cider vinegar

8 red or white radishes, thinly sliced (about 1 cup)

¹/₂ head red cabbage, halved and thinly sliced crosswise (about 3 cups)

Fish

¹/₄ cup fresh lime juice (2–3 limes)

3 tablespoons plus 2 teaspoons extra-virgin olive oil

2 tablespoons finely chopped cilantro

¹/₂ teaspoon ground cumin

¹/₂ teaspoon cayenne

¹/₄ teaspoon sea salt

1¹/₂ pounds mahi-mahi or tilapia fillets, or 1¹/₂ pounds peeled and deveined medium shrimp

Sauce

¹/₂ cup nonfat plain Greek yogurt

2 tablespoons good-quality tequila (you can substitute additional lime juice if you prefer)

1 teaspoon grated lime zest

1 tablespoon fresh lime juice

1 teaspoon finely chopped cilantro

Tacos

2 teaspoons canola oil

12 corn tortillas (6-inch diameter)

2 limes, cut into wedges

1 avocado, peeled and sliced; optional

To make the slaw: Whisk the sugar and vinegar together in a medium bowl. Add the radishes and cabbage, cover tightly with plastic wrap, and refrigerate for at least 3 hours and preferably overnight.

(continued)

To marinate the fish: Whisk the lime juice, olive oil, cilantro, cumin, cayenne, and salt together in a medium bowl. Add the fish fillets and turn to coat. Cover the bowl with plastic wrap and refrigerate for at least 1 hour or up to 3 hours.

To make the sauce: Whisk the yogurt, tequila, lime zest, lime juice, and cilantro together in a small bowl. Cover with plastic wrap and refrigerate until serving.

To make the tacos: Preheat a grill to high, or heat a ridged cast iron grill pan over high heat. Use paper towels and tongs to grease the grill grates or grill pan with the canola oil. Remove the fish from the marinade and grill, without turning, until firm and opaque throughout, 4 to 5 minutes. Transfer the fish to a plate and break it up into bite-size pieces.

Stack the tortillas and wrap them in damp paper towels. Place them on a plate and microwave in 10-second intervals (about 30 seconds total), checking them between intervals to see if they are warmed through and pliable.

To serve, divide the fish among the tortillas. Top with some pickled slaw and avocado slices, if desired. Serve with the tequila sauce and a fresh lime wedge.

Per serving (without avocado): 470 calories, 13 g fat (1.5 g saturated, 0 g trans), 25 g protein, 4 g fiber, 28 g sugars, 269 mg sodium, 61 g carbohydrates, 83 mg cholesterol

CHAPTER 7

Lean Machine Protein

When it comes to protein, be it chicken, turkey, or a big juicy steak, I always keep my big sister's mantra in mind: "Meat is a treat." Proteins are really important, but you don't need to overdo them. To keep the dish as trim as possible, always pair them with healthy whole grains, beans, and loads of veggies. An easy way to do this is to bump the meat from the center of the plate to side dish status and bulk up the healthier options so they drive the plate. In this chapter, you'll find a lots of delicious examples of how to revamp your dinner plate.

Thinking ahead really pays off when you're making this recipe. Letting the chicken hang out with the rub overnight gives it tons of big, deep flavor so you can throw these fresh and filling fajitas together in under 30 minutes. FWB: Spinach, black beans

Chicken Fajitas with Caliente Rub

SERVES **4**

Chicken and rub

1 teaspoon cayenne

1 teaspoon chipotle chile powder

1 tablespoon dried oregano

$\frac{1}{2}$ teaspoon garlic powder

$\frac{1}{2}$ teaspoon sea salt

$\frac{3}{4}$ pound boneless, skinless chicken breasts, cut crosswise into $\frac{1}{2}$-inch-wide strips

Fajitas

1 tablespoon canola oil

1 medium onion, halved and sliced

1 red bell pepper, thinly sliced

1 cup chopped spinach

$\frac{1}{2}$ cup canned black beans, rinsed and drained

4 low-fat whole wheat tortillas (8-inch diameter)

$\frac{1}{4}$ cup salsa

$\frac{1}{4}$ cup nonfat plain Greek yogurt

1 lime, cut into wedges

To marinate the chicken: Stir the cayenne, chile powder, oregano, garlic powder, and salt together in a small bowl. Place the chicken in a quart-size resealable plastic bag along with half of the caliente rub, working the spices into the chicken. Seal and refrigerate the chicken for at least 1 hour or overnight.

To make the fajitas: Heat the oil in a large skillet over medium-high heat. Add the onion and cook, stirring occasionally, until they're soft and browned, about 4 minutes. Stir in the bell pepper and the remaining caliente rub and cook, stirring often, until the pepper is soft, about 4 minutes. Add the chicken strips to the pan, reduce the heat to medium, and cook, stirring often, until the strips are cooked through, 10 to 12 minutes. Add the spinach and beans and cook until the spinach is wilted and the beans are warmed through, 2 to 3 minutes. Turn off the heat.

Stack the tortillas and wrap them in a single layer of dampened paper towels. Place the stack on a plate and microwave in 10-second intervals until they're warm, 40 seconds to 1 minute.

Divide the filling among the tortillas. Top each with 1 tablespoon of salsa and 1 tablespoon of yogurt. Serve with a lime wedge.

Per serving: 319 calories, 6 g fat (0.5 g saturated, 0 g trans), 28 g protein, 6 g fiber, 5 g sugars, 796 mg sodium, 39 g carbohydrates, 49 mg cholesterol

Splurge on This!

Like a pair of gorgeous stilettos, there are a few ingredients that I can't live without. They may not be the cheapest items, but they deliver big, either in flavor or nutrients (or both!). Here's a list of my splurge-worthy pantry musts:

Real Parmigiano-Reggiano cheese: A little bit goes a long way.

Fresh herbs: Grow your own to save cash!

Dark sesame oil: Just a drizzle adds a nutty richness to tofu and veggies.

Almonds, cashews, and walnuts: They're pricey, but they're loaded with protein and small amounts of omega-3s and are a good alternative to animal protein.

Truffle oil: Turns the simplest baked potato or roasted vegetables into a treat—worth every penny!

Honey and maple syrup: Sugar from nature has more antioxidants than refined sugar.

Good-quality dark chocolate: There's no substitute for really great chocolate.

Good-quality wine: Only cook with what you wouldn't be embarrassed to serve with the meal!

Real saffron: Just a pinch turns rice or a simple chicken dish into something exotic.

Sea salt: Includes minerals and trace elements that refined salts lack.

Shiitakes, dried or fresh: Dried are cheaper and you can use the soaking liquid like you would chicken broth!

Pot pie is one of the most classic comfort food dishes around and I love it. It's just the OMG-did-I-just-eat-that! aftereffect that I can do without. So here's my veggie-loaded cure for a pot-pie craving. Loaded with tender chicken thigh meat and topped with flaky puff pastry, it's warm, hearty, and dee-lish! FWB: Sweet Potatoes

Hearty Veggie and Chicken Pot Pie

SERVES 8

1 tablespoon canola or extra-virgin olive oil

2 medium parsnips, peeled and finely chopped

1 small onion, finely chopped

8 ounces white mushrooms, quartered

3 garlic cloves, finely minced

2 pounds boneless, skinless chicken thighs, cut into $\frac{1}{2}$-inch pieces

$\frac{1}{4}$ cup all-purpose flour, sifted

$1\frac{1}{2}$ cups low-sodium chicken broth

$1\frac{1}{2}$ pounds (about 2) large sweet potatoes, chopped into $\frac{1}{2}$-inch cubes

2 sprigs fresh thyme plus 1 teaspoon finely chopped thyme leaves

$\frac{3}{4}$ teaspoon sea salt

1 egg, beaten for an egg wash

1 large sheet frozen puff pastry, thawed

Fresh sage leaves (optional)

Lightly coat the sides and top edge of a 9 × 13-inch baking dish or eight 8-ounce ramekins with cooking spray and set aside. Preheat the oven to 350°F.

Heat the oil in a large pot over medium heat. Stir in the parsnips and onion and cook until they soften, about 3 minutes. Add the mushrooms and cook, stirring occasionally, until they release their liquid, about 5 minutes. Stir in the garlic and cook until it is fragrant, about 1 minute.

Add the chicken and cook until opaque, 5 to 7 minutes. Lightly dust the chicken and vegetables with the sifted flour and gently toss to coat. Add the sweet potatoes, thyme sprigs, and $\frac{1}{2}$ teaspoon of the salt. Pour in a little of the broth, stirring and scraping any browned bits off the bottom of the pot, and then pour in the remaining broth. Reduce the heat to medium-low, cover, and cook, stirring occasionally, until the sweet potatoes are tender and the sauce is thick, about 20 minutes.

Transfer the hot filling to the prepared baking dish. Unfold the puff pastry sheet and use a rolling pin to roll out to a rectangle just slightly larger than your baking dish. If using ramekins, cut the pastry into 8 squares and roll out as needed to cover the tops. Gently place the pastry over the filling, using a rubber spatula to

(continued)

tuck in the sides. Brush with the egg wash and sprinkle with the remaining $\frac{1}{4}$ teaspoon of salt and chopped thyme. If desired, decorate the top with whole sage leaves.

If using ramekins, place them on a baking sheet.

Bake until the top is golden brown, about 20 minutes; ramekins will be done a bit earlier, so check after 10 minutes or so. Let the pot pie (or pies) rest at least 10 minutes before serving.

Per serving: 293 calories, 9 g fat (1.4 g saturated, 0 g trans), 20 g protein, 5 g fiber, 7 g sugars, 326 mg sodium, 33 g carbohydrates, 65 mg cholesterol

♥ Frugal & Fab
Pot pie is a perfect way to revamp leftover chicken or turkey. Instead of browning the meat, just add it to the filling after it has simmered for 20 minutes. Quick, easy, and definitely a money saver.

A simple and dee-lish company dinner, this pairs flavorful chicken thighs with quinoa, an incredible alternative to rice or pasta. If you don't know quinoa, then it's time to. Not only is it high in protein, it's a complete protein, meaning it delivers all nine essential amino acids. It also cooks up light and fluffy and has a fab nutty flavor. FWB: Quinoa, dried cranberries

Apricot Chicken with Quinoa-Almond Pilaf

SERVES 6

Chicken

$1/2$ cup apricot preserves

2 tablespoons Dijon mustard

2 tablespoons reduced-sodium soy sauce

$1/2$ teaspoon sea salt

$1/4$ teaspoon cayenne

$1/4$ teaspoon garlic powder

2 pounds skinless, boneless chicken thighs

Pilaf

1 box (12 ounces) quinoa (about 2 cups)

2 cups low-sodium chicken broth

2 tablespoons balsamic vinegar

1 tablespoon extra-virgin olive oil

$1/2$ teaspoon sea salt

$1/2$ teaspoon ground black pepper

$1/2$ cup dried cranberries

$1/2$ cup finely chopped fresh basil leaves

$1/2$ cup sliced almonds

To marinate the chicken: Whisk the preserves, mustard, soy sauce, salt, cayenne, and garlic powder together in a glass baking dish. Add the chicken and turn to coat in the marinade. Cover with plastic wrap and refrigerate for at least 1 hour or overnight, turning the chicken occasionally.

To make the pilaf: Place the quinoa in a large bowl, cover with cold water, and then drain through a fine-mesh sieve. Place the quinoa, chicken broth, and 2 cups of water in a medium saucepan and bring to a boil over high heat. Reduce the heat to low and simmer uncovered until the quinoa is tender and has absorbed the liquid, 12 to 15 minutes. Scrape the quinoa into a large bowl. Whisk the balsamic vinegar, olive oil, salt, and pepper together in a medium bowl. Add to the quinoa with the cranberries and basil and toss to coat.

Preheat the oven to 350°F. Place the almonds on a rimmed baking sheet and bake until golden and fragrant, 6 to 8 minutes. Transfer the almonds to a large plate to cool. Leave the oven on.

Place the dish with the chicken and marinade in the oven and bake until the chicken is golden and cooked through, 25 to 30 minutes.

Serve the apricot chicken with the pilaf, sprinkled with the toasted almonds.

Per serving: 514 calories, 14 g fat (2 g saturated, 0 g trans), 32 g protein, 6 g fiber, 19 g sugars, 703 mg sodium, 66 g carbohydrates, 87 mg cholesterol

What is it about peanut sauce that makes everyone drool, especially when paired with noodles? I make peace with the carbs in the noodles and the sauce by following this simple equation: Combine two-thirds veggies and protein with one-third good carbs (like whole wheat noodles) and you're not in danger of overloading on starch and sugars. Save some for lunch tomorrow. FWB: Shiitake mushrooms, whole wheat spaghetti

Easy-Peasy Peanut Noodles with Chicken

SERVES **4**

½ pound whole wheat spaghetti

1½ teaspoons sea salt

1 tablespoon dark sesame oil

¾ pound boneless, skinless chicken breasts, cut crosswise into ½-inch-wide strips

1½ tablespoons grated fresh ginger

3 garlic cloves, finely minced

Heaping ¼ cup creamy natural peanut butter

3 tablespoons honey

3 tablespoons reduced-sodium soy sauce

¾ teaspoon red-pepper flakes

1 cup sliced shiitake mushroom caps or ½ cup dried shiitake mushrooms soaked in boiling water for 5 minutes, drained, and chopped

1 red bell pepper, halved and thinly sliced

1 large zucchini, halved lengthwise and thinly sliced crosswise

3 scallions, cut into strips

Bring a large pot of water to a boil. Add the pasta and salt and cook until al dente, 8 to 10 minutes. Scoop out ¼ cup of the pasta cooking water and then drain the pasta in a colander. Rinse the pasta under cold running water for a minute or two to chill the noodles. Give them a few shakes to remove the excess water and set aside.

Heat the sesame oil in a large, deep nonstick skillet over medium heat. Add the chicken and cook, stirring often, until golden brown on all sides and cooked through, about 8 minutes. Transfer the chicken to a plate and set aside.

Add the ginger and garlic to the pan and cook, stirring often, until fragrant, about 1 minute. Stir in the peanut butter, honey, soy sauce, red-pepper flakes, and reserved pasta cooking water and cook until creamy, about 2 minutes. Add the mushrooms, bell pepper, and zucchini. Cook, stirring often, until the vegetables are tender, 2 to 3 minutes. Stir in the cooked chicken and drained noodles and serve sprinkled with the scallions.

Per serving: 536 calories, 14 g fat (2 g saturated, 0 g trans), 35 g protein, 11 g fiber, 20 g sugars, 962 mg sodium, 72 g carbohydrates, 49 mg cholesterol

Isn't it high time we all started thinking outside the Chinese takeout box? Orange chicken has got to be the number-one most popular Chinese dish—and perhaps one of the least healthy too. I make it over by stir-frying instead of deep-frying and using lots of yummy flavors like orange juice and ground ginger. I pair it with fiber-filled brown rice, so there's no chance you'll be hungry an hour after eating it. FWB: Brown rice

Orange-Glazed Chicken Stir-Fry over Brown Rice

SERVES 4

1 cup brown rice

1 cup orange juice (preferably freshly squeezed from 2–3 oranges)

2 tablespoons honey

2 tablespoons reduced-sodium soy sauce

1 teaspoon garlic powder

1 teaspoon ground ginger

1 teaspoon cayenne

1 tablespoon dark sesame oil

3/4 pound boneless, skinless chicken breasts, cut into 1/2-inch cubes

1 cup sliced shiitake mushroom caps or 1/2 cup dried shiitake mushrooms covered in boiling waters for 5 minutes, drained, and chopped

1 cup snow peas, trimmed

1/2 cup canned baby corn, rinsed and drained

Bring 2 1/2 cups of water to a simmer in a medium saucepan. Add the rice, reduce the heat to low, cover, and cook until it has completely absorbed the water and is cooked through yet still retains a bit of chew, about 40 minutes. Turn off the heat and leave covered until serving.

Place the orange juice, honey, soy sauce, garlic powder, ginger, and cayenne in a small saucepan and bring to a simmer. Reduce the heat to medium-low and simmer gently until the sauce is thick and syrupy, 20 to 25 minutes. Turn off the heat and set aside.

Heat the sesame oil in a large nonskillet over medium-high heat. Add the chicken and cook until all sides are golden, stirring occasionally, about 8 minutes. Add the mushrooms, snow peas, and baby corn and cook until the snow peas are tender, about 5 minutes. Stir in the orange sauce and toss to coat. Serve over the brown rice.

Per serving: 448 calories, 7 g fat (1 g saturated, 0 g trans), 30 g protein, 5 g fiber, 16 g sugars, 430 mg sodium, 67 g carbohydrates, 50 mg cholesterol

♡Frugal & Fab

Save *money* by purchasing brown rice in bulk, and save *time* by cooking up a big batch of it on Sundays—it will keep just fine in the fridge 'til Friday.

Boneless, skinless chicken breasts are an absolute freezer staple at my house. I load up when they're on sale and cook them at least twice a week. Everyone loves chicken fingers and this is a more adult take on the childhood favorite.

Sesame-Ginger Chicken Strips with Tangy Marmalade Dip

SERVES 6

Chicken

½ cup reduced-sodium soy sauce

2 tablespoons dark sesame oil

1 tablespoon grated fresh ginger

3 garlic cloves, finely minced

2 pounds boneless, skinless chicken breasts, cut crosswise into ½-inch-wide strips

1 tablespoon sesame seeds

1¼ cups panko bread crumbs

Dip

½ cup orange marmalade

2 tablespoons Dijon mustard

1 tablespoon fresh lime juice

1 tablespoon reduced-sodium soy sauce

¼ cup finely chopped fresh cilantro

To prepare the chicken: Place the soy sauce, sesame oil, ginger, and garlic in a gallon-size resealable plastic bag. Seal the bag and shake the marinade ingredients together. Add the chicken, seal the bag, and shake to coat. Refrigerate for at least 1 hour or overnight.

Preheat the oven to 375°F. Line an 18 × 13-inch rimmed baking sheet with foil and lightly coat the foil with cooking spray.

Place the sesame seeds in a small skillet and heat over medium heat, shaking the pan often, until fragrant and toasty, 1 to 2 minutes. Place the panko and sesame seeds in a shallow bowl. Add the chicken strips and turn to coat, making sure they are all covered with an even layer of bread crumbs. Arrange the chicken on the baking sheet in a single layer. Bake until the chicken is cooked through and the panko is golden, about 20 minutes, turning the strips midway through cooking.

To make the dip: Whisk the marmalade, mustard, lime juice, soy sauce, and cilantro together in a small bowl. Serve the chicken strips with the marmalade-mustard dip.

Per serving: 326 calories, 5 g fat (1 g saturated, 0 g trans), 38 g protein, 1 g fiber, 16 g sugars, 748 mg sodium, 29 g carbohydrates, 88 mg cholesterol

Yes, that's right, chicken and waffles! This is quite possibly the most comforting comfort food—warm, tender, brittle-around-the-edges waffles topped with deliciously crisp baked chicken and finished with a drizzle of real maple syrup. Soul food to the nth degree, this recipe satisfies on the deepest level and is a healthier choice than other fat-packed comfort favorites. FWB: Whole wheat flour

Maple Chicken and Waffles

SERVES **4**

Chicken

$^{1}/_{2}$ cup low-fat buttermilk

$^{1}/_{4}$ cup maple syrup plus $^{1}/_{3}$ cup for serving

2 pounds boneless, skinless chicken breasts

$^{1}/_{2}$ cup panko bread crumbs

$^{1}/_{4}$ teaspoon ground cinnamon

$^{1}/_{4}$ teaspoon freshly grated nutmeg

$^{1}/_{4}$ teaspoon sea salt

Waffles

$1^{1}/_{2}$ cups whole wheat flour

2 tablespoons light brown sugar

$1^{1}/_{2}$ teaspoons baking soda

$^{1}/_{2}$ teaspoon sea salt

$^{3}/_{4}$ teaspoon ground cinnamon

$^{1}/_{4}$ teaspoon freshly grated nutmeg

1 cup low-fat buttermilk

2 large eggs

To make the chicken: Whisk the buttermilk and $^{1}/_{4}$ cup of the maple syrup together in a medium bowl. Add the chicken and turn to coat. Cover the bowl with plastic wrap and refrigerate for 1 hour or overnight.

Preheat the oven to 400°F. Line a rimmed baking sheet with foil and lightly coat the foil with cooking spray.

Stir together the panko, cinnamon, nutmeg, and salt in a medium bowl. Remove the chicken from the marinade, letting the excess drip back into the bowl. Place the chicken breasts in the bread crumbs and turn to coat so each side is evenly covered with seasoned panko. Set the chicken on the baking sheet and bake until the coating is golden and crispy and the chicken is cooked through, about 30 minutes. Leave the oven on, but reduce the temperature to 250°F. When the chicken is cool enough to handle, slice crosswise into thin strips.

To make the waffles: Whisk the flour, brown sugar, baking soda, salt, cinnamon, and nutmeg together in a large bowl. Whisk the buttermilk and eggs together in a medium bowl. Add the buttermilk mixture to the flour mixture, and stir together until just combined.

(continued)

Heat a waffle iron according to the manufacturer's instructions. Coat the iron with cooking spray and then add enough batter to fill the holes without overflowing once the iron is closed. Cook until gorgeous and browned. As the waffles are made, place them on a baking sheet and place in the 250° oven to stay warm while you cook the rest.

To serve, stack 1 or 2 waffles on a plate (depending on how hungry you are). Criss-cross the chicken strips over the waffles, drizzle with a little of the maple syrup, and serve extra on the side.

Per serving (2 waffles): 566 calories, 7 g fat (2.2 g saturated, 0 g trans), 65 g protein, 6 g fiber, 20 g sugars, 963 mg sodium, 59 g carbohydrates, 241 mg cholesterol

♥ Frugal & Fab

DIY waffles are leaner on the waistline and the wallet. Wrap leftovers in plastic wrap and freeze in a gallon-size resealable freezer bag for up to 3 months. Reheat in a toaster, toaster oven, or on a baking sheet under a broiler for fresh and crisp homemade waffles in a healthy heartbeat.

Quinoa is definitely my wingman of choice when it comes to partnering a grain with a protein. Unlike white rice, pasta, or couscous, quinoa delivers all nine essential amino acids as well as a nutty flavor and fluffy texture; plus it's filling and cooks quickly. Show it some love and it'll love you right back. FWB: Spinach, quinoa

Olive Oil–Grilled Chicken over Quinoa-Spinach Salad

SERVES **4**

2 boneless, skinless chicken breast halves (6 ounces each)

2 tablespoons extra-virgin olive oil

$^3/_4$ teaspoon sea salt

$^1/_2$ teaspoon ground black pepper

1 cup quinoa

3 tablespoons sherry vinegar

1 tablespoon Dijon mustard

1 large bunch spinach, ends trimmed, leaves roughly chopped

1 large sweet-tart apple (like Granny Smith or Fuji), halved and thinly sliced

$^1/_2$ cup walnuts

$^1/_2$ cup dried cranberries

Brush the chicken with 2 teaspoons of the olive oil and season with $^1/_2$ teaspoon of the salt and $^1/_4$ teaspoon of the pepper. Heat a ridged cast iron grill pan over medium heat. Brush the grill ridges with 1 teaspoon of the olive oil and brown the chicken on both sides until golden and cooked through, 8 to 10 minutes total. Transfer the chicken to a plate to cool and then slice crosswise into thin strips.

Place the quinoa in a large bowl, cover with cold water, and then drain through a sieve. Place the quinoa in a medium saucepan with 2 cups of water and bring to a boil over high heat. Reduce the heat to low and simmer uncovered until the quinoa is tender and has absorbed the liquid, 12 to 15 minutes.

Whisk the vinegar, mustard, and the remaining 1 tablespoon olive oil, $^1/_4$ teaspoon salt, and $^1/_4$ teaspoon pepper together in a small bowl and set aside.

To make the salad, toss the spinach with the apple, walnuts, and cranberries in a large bowl. Place a scoop of quinoa on each plate and spoon some of the spinach salad on top. Add a few chicken strips. Drizzle with a little dressing and serve the remaining dressing on the side.

Per serving: 480 calories, 19 g fat (2.4 g saturated, 0 g trans), 30 g protein, 7 g fiber, 14 g sugars, 50 mg sodium, 49 g carbohydrates, 49 mg cholesterol

Teri-Glazed Turkey Meatball Yakitori

SERVES **6**

Glaze

¼ cup honey

2 tablespoons reduced-sodium soy sauce

1 teaspoon ground ginger

1 teaspoon garlic powder

Yakitori

1½ tablespoons sesame seeds

1 large egg

1 pound lean ground turkey

½ cup panko bread crumbs

16 scallions, finely chopped

8 garlic cloves, finely minced

2 tablespoons reduced-sodium soy sauce

1 tablespoon dark sesame oil

2 teaspoons sea salt

1 teaspoon ground black pepper

To make the glaze: Whisk the honey, soy sauce, ginger, and garlic together in a small bowl and set aside.

To make the yakitori: Soak twenty-four 6-inch bamboo skewers in warm water for 20 minutes.

Toast the sesame seeds in a small skillet over medium heat, shaking the pan often, until they are fragrant and nutty, 1 to 2 minutes. Transfer the seeds to a small plate and set aside to cool.

Lightly beat the egg in a large bowl. Add the turkey, panko, scallions, garlic, soy sauce, sesame oil, toasted sesame seeds, salt, and pepper. Form the meat mixture into 24 football-shaped torpedos, and thread one onto each skewer.

Heat a ridged cast iron grill pan to medium-high and coat with cooking spray. Grill the skewers in batches until browned on one side, about 4 minutes. Turn the skewers, brush the cooked side with some of the glaze, and grill 4 minutes to brown the second side. Turn the skewers and brush with more glaze.

Pile the skewers onto a platter and let them rest for a few minutes. Drizzle with the remaining glaze and serve hot.

Per serving: 223 calories, 6 g fat (1 g saturated, 0 g trans), 23 g protein, 2 g fiber, 13 g sugars, 985 mg sodium, 21 g carbohydrates, 65 mg cholesterol

Anyone from Cali is going to recognize this totally Hollywood burger (translation: healthy, unique, and stylish!). Pair it with the Beverly Hills Fries (page 206) for a truly Left Coast experience. This recipe makes great mini burgers, too! FWB: Mushrooms, ground turkey

The Hollywood Burger

SERVES **4**

2 tablespoons extra-virgin olive oil or canola oil

1 yellow onion, finely chopped

8 ounces button mushrooms, stemmed and thinly sliced

1 teaspoon sea salt

1 pound lean ground turkey (preferably white meat)

¼ cup panko bread crumbs

2 tablespoons finely chopped flat-leaf parsley

2 tablespoons Worcestershire sauce

½ cup Skinny 'Cue Sauce (page 176)

½ teaspoon ground black pepper

2 tablespoons Dijon mustard

1½ teaspoons honey

12 large Bibb lettuce leaves

1 tomato, sliced

½ Hass avocado, thinly sliced

Heat 1 tablespoon of the oil in a large nonstick skillet over medium-high heat. Add the onion and cook, stirring occasionally, until starting to soften, about 3 minutes. Stir in the mushrooms and cook, stirring often, until they release their moisture, 2 to 3 minutes. Mix in ½ teaspoon of the salt, reduce the heat to medium-low, cover, and cook, stirring occasionally, until the mixture is deep brown and sticky, about 10 minutes (if the mixture is getting too dark too quickly, reduce the heat to low). Transfer the caramelized onion and mushrooms to a small bowl and set aside to cool. Wipe out the skillet and set aside (you'll use it to cook the burgers).

Combine the turkey, panko, parsley, Worcestershire sauce, 1 tablespoon of the Skinny 'Cue Sauce, the pepper, the remaining ½ teaspoon salt, and the caramelized onions and mushrooms in a large bowl. Mix together until combined. Form into patties.

Heat the remaining 1 tablespoon oil in the nonstick skillet over medium-high heat. Add the burgers and cook until browned on both sides and cooked through, about 10 minutes total. Using a spatula, transfer the burgers to a large plate and set aside to rest for 5 minutes (this keeps them nice and juicy!).

(*continued*)

Part of being frugal and fabulous is knowing when to buy and when to hold—and when lean ground turkey is on sale, you want to buy, buy, buy! Store it in your freezer (repackage the turkey in a vacuum-sealed bag or in a triple layer of plastic wrap and then in a freezer bag) and defrost in your microwave or overnight in your fridge.

Whisk the mustard and honey together and set aside. Slightly overlap 2 lettuce leaves on a plate. Set the burger on the lettuce. Add a generous tablespoon of honey-mustard. Cover with a tomato slice, an avocado slice or two, and 2 tablespoons of the Skinny 'Cue Sauce. Top with another lettuce leaf and serve immediately! (If you didn't already guess, this is an eat-with-your-hands-style burger, so be sure to serve up with a nice, absorbent cloth napkin.)

Per serving: 341 calories, 12 g fat (1 g saturated, 0 g trans), 32 g protein, 4 g fiber, 18 g sugars, 958 mg sodium, 30 g carbohydrates, 45 mg cholesterol

Why buy premade barbecue sauce when you already have all of the ingredients in your fridge and pantry? Say bye-bye to nasty preservatives, sugars, and unnecessary calories and hello to big flavor that gives burgers and baked chicken a boost.

Skinny 'Cue Sauce

MAKES ABOUT ¾ CUP

½ cup tomato paste

2 tablespoons honey

2 tablespoons fresh orange juice

1 tablespoon dark brown sugar

2 teaspoons Dijon mustard

1 teaspoon balsamic vinegar

1 tablespoon smoked paprika

1 teaspoon garlic powder

Whisk together and refrigerate for up to 2 weeks. Donezo!

Per tablespoon: 29 calories, 0 g fat (0 g saturated, 0 g trans), 1 g protein, 1 g fiber, 6 g sugars, 107 mg sodium, 7 g carbohydrates, 0 mg cholesterol

When I'm at a loss for what to make for dinner, I turn to these beefy skewers on a stick. They stretch an already inexpensive top sirloin steak (I have found it for as little as $2.49 a pound—what a steal!) by slicing it into long, thin strips, perfect for threading on bamboo skewers. They're excellent for one, two, or a dozen people. In fact, you can keep some beef frozen in marinade for a last-minute entertaining. Ta-da! FWB: Lean beef

Fab Ginger-Beef Skewers

SERVES 4

¼ cup reduced-sodium soy sauce

2 tablespoons plus 1 teaspoon dark sesame oil

2 tablespoons rice vinegar

1 tablespoon grated fresh ginger

2 garlic cloves, finely minced

1 pound top sirloin steak, sliced crosswise into ½-inch-wide strips

4 scallions, thinly sliced on the diagonal

1 tablespoon sesame seeds, toasted, or Asian Almonds (page 55)

Soak sixteen 8-inch wooden skewers in warm water for 30 minutes.

Place the soy sauce, 2 tablespoons of the sesame oil, the vinegar, ginger, and garlic in a gallon-size resealable plastic bag (or large bowl). Seal and vigorously shake (or whisk) to combine. Add the beef, seal the bag (or cover the bowl with plastic wrap), and refrigerate for at least 1 hour or overnight.

Line a rimmed baking sheet with foil. Drain off the marinade and thread 2 pieces of steak on each skewer. Place the skewers on the baking sheet.

Heat a grill pan over high heat (or heat a grill to high). Using a silicone brush, grease the grill with the remaining 1 teaspoon sesame oil. Grill the beef until browned on both sides, about 4 minutes total (you'll probably have to cook the skewers in 3 or 4 batches unless you're grilling them on a big grill). Use tongs to transfer them to a plate and let them rest for 5 minutes before serving sprinkled with the scallions and sesame seeds.

Per serving: 207 calories, 10 g fat (2.5 g saturated, 0 g trans), 26 g protein, 1 g fiber, 0 g sugars, 359 mg sodium, 2 g carbohydrates, 53 mg cholesterol

There's a "manwich," so why not a man-salad? This dinner has Popeye appeal to the max, with protein-rich spinach and steak plus the bold flavor of blue cheese and the crunch of walnuts. It's one of my favorite ways to beef up my iron stores while staying lean and mean. FWB: Spinach, quinoa

Steak Man-Salad

SERVES 6

1 pound lean sirloin steak

1 teaspoon garlic powder

½ teaspoon cayenne

2 teaspoons sea salt

2 cups quinoa

1 teaspoon plus 2 tablespoons extra-virgin olive oil

3 tablespoons fresh lemon juice

1 bunch fresh spinach, ends trimmed (leaves coarsely chopped if large)

1 summer squash, peeled into ribbons with a vegetable peeler

½ cup dried cranberries

¼ cup walnuts, raw or toasted

2 tablespoons blue cheese (optional)

♡ Frugal & Fab

Save up your steak dinners for when your store offers sirloin steaks on sale—often for just $2 to $3 a pound—not bad for steak for four!

Sprinkle the steak all over with the garlic powder, cayenne, and 1 teaspoon of the salt. Cover with plastic wrap and refrigerate for 30 minutes.

While the steak marinates, place the quinoa in a large bowl, cover with cold water, and then drain through a sieve. Place the quinoa, 4 cups of water, and ½ teaspoon of the salt in a medium saucepan and bring to a boil over high heat. Reduce the heat to low and simmer uncovered until the quinoa is tender and has absorbed the liquid, 12 to 15 minutes.

Heat a ridged cast iron grill pan over high heat (or heat a grill to high heat). Using a silicone brush, grease the grill with 1 teaspoon of the olive oil. Add the steak and sear until nicely browned, about 4 minutes per side for medium-rare. Let rest on a cutting board for 5 minutes before slicing it thinly across the grain.

Whisk the lemon juice, remaining 2 tablespoons olive oil, and remaining 1 teaspoon salt together in a small bowl. Add the spinach, squash ribbons, cranberries, walnuts, and lemon vinaigrette to the still-warm quinoa and toss to combine. The spinach should wilt slightly. Divide the quinoa and steak among 4 plates. Sprinkle with blue cheese, if desired, and serve.

Per serving: 449 calories, 18 g fat (4 g saturated, 0 g trans), 24 g protein, 7 g fiber, 8 g sugars, 616 mg sodium, 50 g carbohydrates, 37 mg cholesterol

The zesty combo of smoked paprika and earthy cumin on a good pan-seared steak is a flavor pair that has become a house fave. The paprika rub is awesome on chicken breasts and lean pork loin, and even for seasoning baked potatoes, squash, and other roasted and baked veggies. I swear, you won't even miss the butter. FWB: Potatoes

Smoky Paprika-Rubbed Sirloin with Zucchini-Stuffed Potatoes

SERVES 6

Steak

1 teaspoon smoked paprika

1 teaspoon garlic powder

1/2 teaspoon ground cumin

1 teaspoon sea salt

2 pounds top sirloin steak

1 teaspoon extra-virgin olive oil

Potatoes

6 medium russet (baking) potatoes

2 tablespoons extra-virgin olive oil

1 teaspoon sea salt

1/2 small onion, thinly sliced

2 garlic cloves, finely minced

1 large or 2 medium zucchini, halved lengthwise and thinly sliced crosswise

To prepare the steak: Stir the smoked paprika, garlic powder, cumin, and salt together in a small bowl. Rub the steak all over with the spices. Wrap the steak in plastic wrap and refrigerate for at least 1 hour or overnight.

To bake the potatoes: Preheat the oven to 350°F. Line a rimmed baking sheet with foil. Pierce the potatoes several times with a fork or metal skewer. Place them in a bowl and toss with 1 tablespoon of the olive oil and the salt. Transfer the potatoes to the baking sheet and bake until a paring knife easily slips into the centers without any resistance, about 1 hour 30 minutes. Set aside to cool slightly. Leave the oven on for the steak.

When the potatoes have been in the oven for 30 minutes, take the steak out of the fridge and let it sit at room temperature for 30 minutes.

Even if you're just cooking for one or two people, make the full recipe of the steak so you have leftovers. They're excellent in a whole wheat pita or on flatbread for a steak sandwich. Hello brown-bag lunch extraordinaire!

Heat a ridged cast iron grill pan over medium-high heat. Using a pastry brush or a crumpled paper towel, brush the hot pan with 1 teaspoon of the olive oil. Place the steak in the pan and cook until both sides are browned and nicely marked from the grill, 5 to 6 minutes per side. Place the pan in the oven and cook the steak until done to your liking (12 to 14 minutes for medium-rare). Transfer the steak to a cutting board and let it rest for 5 minutes before thinly slicing across the grain.

Once the steak goes into the oven, heat the remaining 1 tablespoon olive oil in a medium skillet over medium heat. Add the onion and cook until soft and browned, about 10 minutes. Stir in the garlic and zucchini and cook until the zucchini is very soft and tender, 12 to 15 minutes. Cut a slit down the center of each potato and pinch the ends to open up the potato. Stuff each with 2 tablespoons of the zucchini mixture. Serve alongside a few slices of the steak.

Per serving: 431 calories, 12 g fat (3 g saturated, 0 g trans), 39 g protein, 4 g fiber, 3 g sugars, 626 mg sodium, 42 g carbohydrates, 64 mg cholesterol

Slow-roasted pork tacos are the best street-food-turned-everyday-food ever! Making them yourself takes a little time, but a pork loin feeds a ton of people, making these excellent bites for when you need to feed many mouths. This homemade version is leaner than the traditional taco truck pork shoulder—13½ grams of fat per 3 ounces versus 4 grams of fat for 3 ounces of pork loin! FWB: Cabbage

Totally Mexi-Cali Carnitas

SERVES 8

3½-pound boneless pork loin roast, external fat trimmed off

1 tablespoon sea salt

1 tablespoon canola oil or vegetable oil

1 medium onion, finely chopped

1 tablespoon chipotle chile powder

1 tablespoon dried oregano

2 teaspoons ground cumin

16 corn tortillas (6-inch diameter)

¼ head red or green cabbage, thinly sliced

Topping "bar" (all are optional—offer as many or few as you like!)

1 Hass avocado, thinly sliced

½ cup nonfat plain Greek yogurt

½ cup coarsely chopped cilantro

½ cup shredded Cotija cheese

Store-bought salsa

Rub the entire surface of the pork loin with the salt. Heat the oil in a heavy-bottomed deep pot or Dutch oven over medium heat. Add the pork and brown on all sides, about 5 minutes per side. Pour in 1 cup water and add the onion, chipotle powder, oregano, and cumin and bring to a boil over high heat. Boil for 4 minutes, then reduce the heat to low, cover, and simmer until the meat is incredibly tender and falls apart easily, about 2 hours, turning a few times while cooking. Turn off the heat and let the roast rest in the pot until it is cool enough to handle, about 30 minutes. Transfer the roast to a cutting board and shred the meat with your fingers or two forks, then return it to the juices in the pan so the lean meat stays nice and moist.

Soak a clean kitchen towel in warm water and wring it dry. Stack the tortillas and place them in the center of the towel. Wrap the towel around the tortillas and place them on a microwaveable plate. Microwave the tortillas in 10-second intervals until the tortillas are warm, fragrant, and very soft.

To assemble a carnita, place about 2 tablespoons of meat in the center of 1 warmed tortilla and cover with some cabbage. Add your choice of toppings. Serve warm.

Per (2-taco) serving (without toppings): 481 calories, 12 g fat (2 g saturated, 0 g trans), 43 g protein, 7 g fiber, 3 g sugars, 843 mg sodium, 47 g carbohydrates, 15 mg cholesterol

I love lamb chops, but man are they expensive. So I whip this recipe out exclusively for date nights. They're totally sexy on the plate, lean, full of bold flavor, and fun to eat with your fingers—all definitely date prerequisites. For an extra-sleek presentation, get your butcher to French the rack, meaning all of the meat is scraped off the bones. I love this with quinoa or the Eggplant, Mushroom, and Spinach Sauté on page 195.

Date-Night Knockout Rack of Lamb

SERVES 2

½ cup panko bread crumbs

2 garlic cloves, finely minced

1 tablespoon finely chopped fresh sage or 1½ teaspoons dried

1 tablespoon finely chopped fresh thyme or 1½ teaspoons dried

¾ teaspoon sea salt

1½ tablespoons extra-virgin olive oil

One 6-bone rack of lamb, Frenched

1½ teaspoons Dijon mustard

♥ Frugal & Fab

Pastry brushes are pricey—instead, go to your local hardware store and buy a small natural-bristle paintbrush. It's a fraction of the price and works great.

Preheat the oven to 450°F.

Toss the panko, garlic, sage, thyme, and ¼ teaspoon of the salt together on a rimmed baking sheet. Drizzle 1½ teaspoons of the olive oil over the mixture and rub it between your palms to incorporate it into the bread crumbs. Set aside.

Rub the entire rack of lamb with the remaining ½ teaspoon salt. Heat the remaining 1 tablespoon olive oil in a large ovenproof skillet (cast iron works great!) over high heat. Place the rack of lamb rounded-side down in the pan and cook until browned, 2 to 3 minutes. Turn over and brown for 2 to 3 minutes on the second side. Use tongs to transfer the lamb to a cutting board.

Using a pastry brush, dab the mustard all over the browned lamb. Press both sides of the lamb in the seasoned panko, making sure to cover the entire surface in an even layer of bread crumbs. Wrap a sheet of foil over the tips of the bones (so they don't burn) and place the rack back in the skillet, bone-side down. Place the skillet in the oven and roast the lamb for 12 to 14 minutes for medium. Let the lamb rest for 10 minutes before using a sharp knife to separate the rack into individual chops. Arrange on plates or a platter and serve.

Per serving: 409 calories, 24 g fat (7 g saturated, 0 g trans), 34 g protein, 1 g fiber, <1 g sugars, 849 mg sodium, 12 g carbohydrates, 103 mg cholesterol

Craving pasta? Go for it! Just reduce the quantity by half and replace that 50 percent with veggies as I did in this recipe, which subs in slender zucchini ribbons for pappardelle pasta. You save calories while adding flavor and nutrition. Brainiac concept, isn't it? Top each serving with a tablespoon of part-skim ricotta for a rich touch. FWB: Zucchini

Lamb Ragù with Zucchini Pappardelle

SERVES **6**

4 teaspoons extra-virgin olive oil

1½ pounds ground lamb

Sea salt

1 medium carrot, finely chopped

1 celery stalk, finely chopped

1 medium onion, finely chopped

1 tablespoon finely chopped fresh rosemary or thyme

1 teaspoon ground cumin

1 tablespoon tomato paste

1 cup dry red wine

1 can (28 ounces) crushed tomatoes in puree

1¼ cups low-sodium chicken broth

12 ounces pappardelle pasta

2 medium zucchini, shaved with a vegetable peeler into long ribbons

¼ teaspoon ground black pepper

3 tablespoons grated Parmesan cheese

¼ cup finely chopped fresh basil

Heat 2 teaspoons of the oil in a large pot over medium-high heat. Add the lamb and ½ teaspoon salt. Cook, stirring often, until golden brown, about 5 minutes. Transfer the lamb to a bowl and discard all but 1 tablespoon of the fat from the pot. Add the carrot, celery, onion, rosemary or thyme, and cumin and cook over medium heat until the onion softens, about 3 minutes.

Stir in the tomato paste and cook for 2 minutes, stirring often. Pour in the wine and cook, stirring occasionally, until it is evaporated, about 5 minutes. Add the tomatoes (with juices), chicken broth, and browned lamb. Stir and bring to a boil. Reduce the heat to medium-low and cook until the ragù is thick, stirring a few times, 25 to 30 minutes. Remove from the heat and set aside.

While the sauce is cooking, bring a large pot of salted water to a boil. Add the pasta and cook until it is al dente, according to package directions. Drain and add to the ragù in the pot.

While the pasta is cooking, heat the remaining 2 teaspoons oil in a large nonstick skillet over medium-high heat. Add the zucchini, pepper, and ¼ teaspoon salt. Cook until the zucchini is pliable, about 3 minutes. Add the zucchini to the pasta and toss together gently. Serve topped with the Parmesan and basil.

Per serving: 677 calories, 32 g fat (13 g saturated, 0 g trans), 31 g protein, 6 g fiber, 3 g sugars, 797 mg sodium, 61 g carbohydrates, 85 mg cholesterol

Ⓥ = vegetarian ⓋⓃ = vegan

CHAPTER 8

Skinny on the Side

Drowning veggies in heavy sauces not only kills their delicious taste, but also adds to your waist. Instead, accent their natural flavors with ingredients that add lots of punch, like roasted garlic, lemon, and a small sprinkle of flavorful cheese. I also have an arsenal of skinny swap-outs that I rely on when I need to whittle down traditional recipes. For example, in my roasted garlic mashed potatoes, I use buttermilk and olive oil instead of butter and cream. It's so luscious and packed with deep potato flavor that I bet you won't even miss the fat. The recipes in this chapter are delish alongside a meaty main, or, for a meat-free and wallet-savvy meal, serve two or three together for a main dish of sides!

Bok choy pulls off the sexy trick of being crunchy on the outside and creamy-tender in the middle. It also has a juicy quality that's super delicious, especially when paired with traditional Asian ingredients like ginger and sesame oil. Bonus: It's simple to cook and elegant to serve. This is gorgeous with the Mega Omega Salmon (page 146). FWB: Bok choy

Ginger-Soy Baby Bok Choy

SERVES **4**

1 cup chicken or vegetable broth

2 tablespoons reduced-sodium soy sauce

1 teaspoon dark sesame oil

1 teaspoon grated fresh ginger

4 bunches baby bok choy, leaves separated and then halved lengthwise

Preheat the oven to 350°F. Whisk the broth, soy sauce, sesame oil, and ginger together in a measuring cup. Pour the marinade into a 9 × 13-inch baking dish and add the bok choy, turning the pieces so they all get coated with the sauce. Set aside for 15 minutes.

Turn all of the bok choy pieces cut-side down in the baking dish. Bake the bok choy until it is cooked to your liking—about 15 minutes for crisp bok choy and 20 minutes for softer bok choy. Serve hot.

Per serving: 29 calories, 1.4 g fat (0 g saturated, 0 g trans), 2 g protein, 1 g fiber, 1 g sugars, 555 mg sodium, 3 g carbohydrates, 0 mg cholesterol

Slim Scoop!

One cup of bok choy has about 20 calories. Yes, 20 calories! You practically burn that off just by chewing!

Mustard greens are a nutritional powerhouse, with nine vitamins, seven minerals, and loads of fiber. Thanks to smoked paprika, a.k.a. *pimentón*, you don't need bacon to make these greens smoky and delicious, it has an amazing woodsy and slightly spicy effect on greens that is totally unbelievable. Trust me, once you've had these greens a few times, you'll start craving them on a regular basis! FWB: Mustard greens

Mustard Greens with Smoky Paprika

SERVES 4

2 pounds mustard greens, tough stems trimmed

1 tablespoon olive oil

1 small yellow onion, finely chopped

1–2 teaspoons smoked paprika (depending on how spicy you like your greens!)

1 teaspoon red-pepper flakes (optional)

½ teaspoon sea salt

1 tablespoon fresh lemon juice

Working in batches, stack the mustard greens, roll them into a thick cigar shape, and slice them crosswise into ½-inch-wide ribbons.

Heat the oil in a large nonstick skillet over medium heat. Add the onion and cook until translucent and soft, stirring often, 5 to 7 minutes. Stir in the smoked paprika, red-pepper flakes (if desired), and salt and then add half of the greens. Cook, using tongs to turn the greens often, until they begin to wilt, about 5 minutes. Add the remaining greens and cook, continuing to turn the greens, until they're very tender, 8 to 10 minutes. Turn off the heat and sprinkle with the lemon juice. Serve hot

Per serving: 99 calories, 4 g fat (0.5 g saturated, 0 g trans), 6 g protein, 8 g fiber, 4 g sugars, 255 mg sodium, 13 g carbohydrates, 0 mg cholesterol

♥ Frugal & Fab

Mustard greens and kale are hardier than the softer greens (like Swiss chard and spinach), so they wilt less and retain more water during cooking, meaning more mass for your cash. A side dish for four that costs just a few bucks to make? Now that's a keeper!

Swiss chard is loaded with vitamin A for bright, gorgeous eyes, vitamin K for strong bones, and antioxidant vitamin C for glowing skin. What's not to love about this sexy green? If you can't find pumpkin seeds, try sunflower seeds. FWB: Swiss chard

Sexy Swiss Chard with Golden Raisins and Pumpkin Seeds

SERVES 6

2 pounds Swiss chard, stem ends trimmed

$^1/_4$ cup raw hulled pumpkin seeds

1 tablespoon extra-virgin olive oil

1 small red onion, halved and thinly sliced

$^1/_2$ teaspoon sea salt

$^1/_2$ cup golden raisins

1 tablespoon fresh lemon juice

Slim Scoop!

I use rainbow chard instead of plain white-stemmed chard whenever I can find it. The green leaves are offset by a beautiful blend of red, pink, orange, and yellow stems. So pretty on the plate!

Place the chard on your cutting board. Use a sharp knife to cut out the colorful stems from the leaves. Slice the stems crosswise into $^1/_4$-inch pieces and place them in a bowl. Working in batches, stack the greens, roll them into a thick cigar shape and slice them crosswise into $^1/_4$-inch-wide ribbons.

Toast the pumpkin seeds in a small skillet over medium heat, shaking the pan often, until fragrant, toasty-brown, and plump, 3 to 4 minutes. Transfer to a small plate to cool and set aside.

Heat the oil in a large nonstick skillet over medium-high heat. Add the onion and salt and cook, stirring often, until it begins to soften, 3 to 4 minutes. Stir in the chard stems and cook until they're starting to soften, about 4 minutes. Add the greens and cook, stirring often, until they begin to wilt, about 4 minutes longer. Stir in the raisins and turn off the heat. Sprinkle with the lemon juice and turn the greens out onto a serving platter. Sprinkle the pumpkin seeds over the top and serve.

Per serving: 128 calories, 5 g fat (1 g saturated, 0 g trans), 5 g protein, 4 g fiber, 12 g sugars, 457 mg sodium, 18 g carbohydrates, 0 mg cholesterol

So economical and good for you, this no-cook throw-and-go side is a skinny secret for looking great. You get protein and B vitamins from the beans *and* money in your pocket. FWB: Beans

No-Cook Balsamic Beans

SERVES 4

2 tablespoons balsamic vinegar

1 tablespoon extra-virgin olive oil

1 tablespoon dried oregano

$^1/_4$ teaspoon sea salt

$^1/_8$ teaspoon ground black pepper

$^1/_2$ lemon

1 small red onion, finely chopped

1 can (15 ounces) chickpeas, rinsed and drained

1 can (15 ounces) kidney beans, rinsed and drained

1 cup green beans, cut into bite-size pieces

Whisk the vinegar, olive oil, oregano, salt, and pepper together in a large bowl. Squeeze in some lemon juice and then add the onion, chickpeas, kidney beans, and green beans. Stir together, cover the bowl with plastic wrap, and marinate for at least 30 minutes or up to a few hours. Serve well chilled.

Per serving: 194 calories, 5 g fat (0.5 g saturated, 0 g trans), 9 g protein, 9 g fiber, 6 g sugars, 430 mg sodium, 29 g carbohydrates, 0 mg cholesterol

Slim Scoop!

Almost any bean works here—black beans, navy beans, pinto beans. Use whatever you have in your pantry. If you happen to have fresh basil or cilantro, toss them in—it adds a gorgeous freshness that can't be beat.

This side dish is one of my absolute favorite one-pan veggie wonders. I let the eggplant and mushrooms soak in a fresh lemon vinaigrette first and then give them a good sear. The contrast of tangy, crumbly feta cheese to the creamy eggplant is so amazing. If you're in the mood for spicy, add a few pinches of red-pepper flakes or cayenne to the vinaigrette before marinating the vegetables. FWB: Eggplant

Eggplant, Mushroom, and Spinach Sauté

SERVES 4

1½ tablespoons fresh lemon juice

3 tablespoons extra-virgin olive oil

1¼ teaspoons sea salt

1 large eggplant (about 1 pound), cut into ¾-inch cubes

6 ounces button mushrooms, stems removed, caps thinly sliced

2 cups chopped spinach or baby spinach

2½ ounces crumbled feta or Cotija cheese (about ⅓ cup)

¼ cup finely chopped fresh basil

Whisk the lemon juice, 2 tablespoons of the olive oil, and 1 teaspoon of the salt together in a large bowl. Add the eggplant and mushrooms, toss to combine, cover the bowl with plastic wrap, and set aside for 30 minutes.

Heat the remaining 1 tablespoon oil in a large nonstick skillet over medium-high heat. Add the eggplant and mushrooms and cook, stirring often, until the vegetables are tender and golden brown, about 10 minutes. Stir in the spinach and the remaining ¼ teaspoon salt. Once the spinach is wilted, 1 to 2 minutes, turn off the heat. Sprinkle with the cheese and basil and serve hot.

Per serving: 183 calories, 15 g fat (4 g saturated, 0 g trans), 5 g protein, 4 g fiber, 5 g sugars, 706 mg sodium, 10 g carbohydrates, 16 mg cholesterol

These mushroom fries are more delicious and way more filling than potato fries. Steaklike portobellos are meaty and juicy and in this recipe have a to-die-for crunch thanks to panko bread crumbs. If you're not a horseradish lover, serve them with the Skinny 'Cue Sauce (page 176). FWB: Mushrooms

Portobello Fries with Creamy Horseradish Dip

SERVES 4

Dip

2 tablespoons light mayonnaise

2 teaspoons prepared horseradish

1 teaspoon Worcestershire sauce

1 teaspoon finely chopped flat-leaf parsley

⅛ teaspoon sea salt

Fries

½ cup panko bread crumbs

2 tablespoons finely chopped flat-leaf parsley

1 teaspoon sea salt

½ teaspoon cayenne

2 large eggs

4 large portobello mushrooms, stems removed

½ cup canola oil or vegetable oil

To make the dip: Whisk the mayonnaise, horseradish, Worcestershire, parsley, and salt together in a small bowl. Cover with plastic wrap and refrigerate until serving.

To make the fries: Preheat the oven to 300°F. Whisk the panko, parsley, salt, and cayenne in a medium bowl. Whisk the eggs in another shallow bowl until blended.

Slice the portobellos into ¼-inch sticks. In small batches, dip the mushroom sticks first in the bowl of eggs, then in the bowl with the panko mixture, gently rolling the mushroom sticks to coat all four sides. Transfer to a plate.

Heat the oil in a large skillet over medium-high heat for 2 to 3 minutes. Add a small mushroom stick to the pan. If lots of little bubbles immediately surround the mushroom, then the oil is ready (if nothing happens, then the oil isn't hot enough). Add about half the sticks and fry until the sticks are golden and crisp on all sides, 4 to 6 minutes total. Transfer the fries to a paper towel–lined baking sheet and keep warm in the oven while you fry the remaining batches.

Per serving: 239 calories, 19 g fat (2.3 g saturated, 0 g trans), 6 g protein, 2 g fiber, 2 g sugars, 587 mg sodium, 11 g carbohydrates, 108 mg cholesterol

A Note on "Bad" Foods

I just don't buy into the concept that foods like chocolate cake, pizza, or french fries are "bad," especially when they taste so delicious! That's why I advocate moderation, not deprivation—fried food included. Yes, frying is not the healthiest way to cook food, but giving in to a special treat in small amounts not only quiets the craving, it also prevents denial-induced overindulging. Remaining in control of your appetite is the key to a healthy weight and mindset.

Artichokes are so fun (and sexy) to eat—peeling off the layers, digging into the heart, and dipping leaves into a creamy, luscious sauce that I lighten by using nonfat Greek yogurt instead of artery-clogging mayo. One thing I never could understand, though, is why everyone gets rid off the stems when they roast artichokes. I mean, that's the good stuff, love! FWB: Low-fat yogurt

Roasted Artichokes with No-Mayo Aioli

SERVES 6

Artichokes

4 large artichokes

2 lemons, 1 halved, 1 sliced

1 tablespoon extra-virgin olive oil

1½ teaspoons roasted garlic (page 208)

1 teaspoon sea salt

Sauce

½ cup nonfat plain Greek yogurt

1 tablespoon roasted garlic (page 208)

1 teaspoon fresh lemon juice

½ teaspoon Worcestershire sauce

To make the artichokes: Preheat the oven to 450°F. Slice off the top one-third of the artichoke. Snap off the thick outer layers of leaves until you get to the pale yellow leaves with pale green tips. Halve the artichokes lengthwise and remove the fibrous choke using a sharp paring knife and a teaspoon. Using a vegetable peeler, pare the tough layer from the stem and base. Rub the cut surfaces with a lemon half to keep it from discoloring. (Squeeze the remaining lemon half to get juice for the sauce.)

Coat a 9 × 13-inch baking dish with the olive oil. Place the artichokes cut-side down in the pan and rub around to coat them with oil. Turn them cut-side up, rub the hearts with the roasted garlic, and sprinkle with the salt. Place the lemon slices in the pan and turn the artichokes cut-sides down again so that each half is resting on top of a lemon slice. Roast the artichokes until an outer leaf comes off easily and the heart is tender, 40 to 45 minutes.

Meanwhile, make the sauce: Whisk together the yogurt, roasted garlic, lemon juice, and Worcestershire sauce in a small bowl.

Place each artichoke half on a small plate and serve with the sauce on the side.

Per serving: 86 calories, 2.5 g fat (0.5 g saturated, 0 g trans), 5 g protein, 6 g fiber, 2 g sugars, 376 mg sodium, 13 g carbohydrates, 0 mg cholesterol

Swap This!

I've been cooking and eating trimmed-down recipes for big-flavor food for more than 10 years. Along the way, I've discovered a few stellar swap-out ingredients that save calories, and probably add flavor too! Now, listen up—some of these ingredients aren't cheap. Use them in small amounts, though, and they pay off big when those jeans look abfab on your bod!

Instead of mayonnaise, use hummus
Savings: 32 calories, 4 fat grams per tablespoon

Instead of oil, use chicken broth
Savings: 123 calories, 14 fat grams per tablespoon

Instead of sour cream, use nonfat Greek yogurt
Savings: 15 calories, 2 fat grams per tablespoon

Instead of heavy cream, uses fat-free evaporated milk
Savings: 40 calories, 6 fat grams per tablespoon

Instead of 1 cup shredded whole milk mozzarella, use ¼ cup grated Parmesan
Savings: 228 calories, 18 fat grams

Instead of creamy ranch dressing, use barbecue sauce
Savings: 47 calories, 8 fat grams per tablespoon

Instead of nacho cheese sauce, use fresh salsa
Savings: 103 calories, 9 fat grams per ¼ cup

Instead of reduced-fat 2% milk, use unsweetened almond milk
Savings: 60 calories, 2.5 fat grams per cup

Instead of shredded whole milk mozzarella cheese, use fresh basil
Savings: 83 calories, 6 fat grams per ¼ cup

Instead of 2 whole eggs, use 6 egg whites
Savings: 48 calories, 9 fat grams

Barley has an earthy, nutty personality with a power-house of a nutritional profile. While I try to cook with only fresh veggies in season, sometimes frozen veggies like edamame and peas are the best-tasting and most pocket-friendly option. FWB: Barley, edamame

Pearled Barley with Peas and Edamame

SERVES 4

1 cup pearled barley

1 cup frozen shelled edamame

1 cup frozen peas

1 cup chopped spinach (preferably fresh, but frozen is okay in a pinch; see Note)

2¼ teaspoons Worcestershire sauce

1½ teaspoons grated lemon zest

1½ tablespoons fresh lemon juice

¼ teaspoon sea salt

Place the barley and 4 cups of water in a medium saucepan. Bring to a boil, reduce the heat to low, cover, and cook until all of the water is nearly absorbed, 25 to 30 minutes. Stir in the edamame and peas and cook, uncovered, until the barley absorbs all of the remaining water, another 5 to 10 minutes.

Turn off the heat, stir in the spinach, and set aside. Whisk the Worcestershire sauce, lemon zest, lemon juice, and salt together in a small bowl. Pour the vinaigrette over the barley, stir to combine, and serve warm or at room temperature.

Note: If using frozen spinach, partially thaw to separate into clumps, and add it when adding the edamame and peas.

Per serving: 260 calories, 2 g fat (0 g saturated, 0 g trans), 11 g protein, 12 g fiber, 3 g sugars, 195 mg sodium, 50 g carbohydrates, 0 mg cholesterol

Slim Scoop!

The coolest thing about barley is that it contains plenty of soluble fiber that feeds friendly bacteria in the digestive tract. These good bacteria keep tummies happy and healthy.

Bonus Ingredients

Stop throwing your hard-earned cash in the trash! Here's a list of tasty morsels you should be eating, not trashing.

Beet tops/radish tops: Use in place of Swiss chard or spinach.

Broccoli stems: Amazing sliced into sticks and used in stir-fries, or blanched and then added to pasta or salad

Carrot and celery tops: Use in place of parsley; fab in a salad!

Chicken trimmings and roasted chicken bones: Save for making chicken broth (see page 86).

Citrus peels: After peeling an orange, save the peel and combine with water in a spray bottle for a natural cleanser.

Egg yolks: Turn them into a nutrient-rich hair serum (see page 247).

Mushroom stems: Save for veggie broth, or finely chop to add texture to soup or stir-fries.

Olive brine or pickle liquid: Add a teaspoon to homemade tartar sauce or salad dressing.

Parmesan rinds: Simmer in soup or tomato sauce; discard before serving.

Shrimp shells: Simmer with water (add aromatics like onions, carrots, a bay leaf, black peppercorns, and herb sprigs for a nice flavor, too) for a fast shellfish broth to freeze and use instead of bottled clam juice in seafood pastas and risotto.

Squeezed lemons: Chop them up and grind them in your garbage disposal to help fight odors.

Stems and twigs from fresh herbs: Tie together and hang them from your showerhead for an aromatherapeutic shower.

Used coffee grounds and egg shells: Supernutritious for compost

While this side is great with salmon, tofu, and chicken, it's really an easy, fast, and healthy meal in its own right. Quinoa is loaded with protein, so why not? While quinoa is my favorite superfood add-in, cooked brown rice is excellent too. Make a big batch of whole grains early in the week and quick throw-together side dishes like this one are a snap. FWB: Asparagus, quinoa

Cremini Mushrooms, Asparagus, and Quinoa

SERVES 6

4 tablespoons Worcestershire sauce

1 tablespoon extra-virgin olive oil

1 teaspoon sea salt

10 ounces cremini mushrooms, stemmed and thinly sliced

1 pound asparagus, tough ends snapped off, chopped

2 cups quinoa

Whisk 2 tablespoons of the Worcestershire sauce, the olive oil, and salt together in a medium bowl. Pour half into another medium bowl. Add the mushrooms to one bowl and the asparagus to the other and gently toss to coat them evenly with the marinade. Set aside for 20 to 30 minutes.

While the vegetables marinate, make the quinoa. Place the quinoa in a large bowl, cover with cold water, and then drain through a sieve. Transfer the quinoa to a medium saucepan, add 4 cups of water, and bring to a boil over high heat. Reduce the heat to low and simmer, covered, until the quinoa is tender and has absorbed the liquid, about 25 minutes.

Heat a large nonstick skillet over medium-high heat. Add the mushrooms and the marinade and cook until tender, about 5 minutes. Stir in the asparagus and its marinade and cook until crisp-tender, 5 to 7 minutes. Stir in the remaining 2 tablespoons Worcestershire sauce. Add the quinoa and cook, stirring often, until the quinoa is warmed through. Serve hot.

Per serving: 261 calories, 6 g fat (1 g saturated, 0 g trans), 10 g protein, 6 g fiber, 3 g sugars, 353 mg sodium, 43 g carbohydrates, 0 mg cholesterol

Bold spice combinations and a hint of sexy exoticness make Middle Eastern cuisine one of my favorites. I add a little nonfat Greek yogurt to this brown rice dish so it's extra luxurious and creamy. That plus a bit of curry powder and a squeeze of fresh lime juice completely transport me from LA to the casbah! FWB: Curry powder

Perfect Persian-Spiced Basmati Rice

SERVES 6

2 cups basmati rice

2 teaspoons extra-virgin olive oil

1 small yellow onion, finely chopped

2 teaspoons good-quality curry powder

$\frac{1}{4}$ cup nonfat plain Greek yogurt

1 tablespoon fresh lime juice

$\frac{1}{2}$ teaspoon sea salt

Bring 4 cups of water to a boil in a large saucepan. Add the rice, return to a boil, and reduce the heat to low so it is barely simmering. Cover the pan and cook until tender, 22 to 24 minutes. Turn off the heat and set aside.

Heat the oil in a large nonstick skillet over medium heat. Add the onion and cook, stirring occasionally, until soft and golden, 3 to 5 minutes. Stir in the curry powder and cooked rice. Add the yogurt, lime juice, and salt, and stir to combine. Turn off the heat and serve hot.

Per serving: 226 calories, 2 g fat (0 g saturated, 0 g trans), 5 g protein, 2 g fiber, 1 g sugars, 135 mg sodium, 46 g carbohydrates, 0 mg cholesterol

Root vegetables like parsnips, rutabagas, and turnips are usually overshadowed by their more colorful cousins, beets, carrots, and sweet potatoes. Because they've fallen a bit out of favor, guess what? These babies are dirt cheap! Everyone should know how to make a side dish of roasted root veggies. The raw vegetables keep for weeks in the fridge or dry pantry, and they taste so, so good when roasting coaxes all of their natural sugars out to play. It's a win-win equation. FWB: Sweet potatoes

One-Dish Roasted Root Veggies

SERVES 6

4 pounds mixed root vegetables (beets, carrots, parsnips, rutabagas, turnips, sweet potatoes), cut into 1-inch chunks

2 shallots, finely chopped

¼ cup finely chopped fresh herbs (basil, oregano, or thyme)

1 teaspoon sea salt

3 tablespoons extra-virgin olive oil

1 tablespoon truffle oil (optional, but fabulous!)

Preheat the oven to 350°F. Place the veggies in a 9 × 13-inch baking dish. Add the shallots, herbs, salt, and olive oil and toss to coat. Roast until all of the vegetables are tender, and a paring knife easily slides into their centers, about 1 hour.

Transfer the veggies to a serving dish and drizzle with truffle oil, if desired. Serve hot.

Per serving: 222 calories, 8 g fat (1 g saturated, 0 g trans), 4 g protein, 8 g fiber, 16 g sugars, 431 mg sodium, 37 g carbohydrates, 0 mg cholesterol

Now I ask you, who doesn't love a heaping pile of french fries? Sweet potato fries roasted to sweet perfection are delicious with just about anything, like the Hollywood Burger on page 174 or even a steak, like the one on page 180. Pair them with the sweet and sharp Skinny 'Cue Sauce (page 176) and you'll rethink America's obsession with ketchup and fries. FWB: Sweet potatoes

Beverly Hills Fries with Honey-'Cue Sauce

SERVES **6**

4 large sweet potatoes, scrubbed
2 teaspoons extra-virgin olive oil
1 teaspoon garlic powder (optional)
3/4 teaspoon sea salt
Skinny 'Cue Sauce (page 176)

Preheat the oven to 450°F. Halve the sweet potatoes lengthwise and cut each half lengthwise into 4 long wedges. Place the sweet potatoes on a rimmed baking sheet. Drizzle the oil over the potatoes, add the garlic powder, if desired, and 1/2 teaspoon of the salt, and toss to coat. Roast the potatoes until golden brown and slightly crisp, 25 to 30 minutes. Sprinkle the potatoes with the remaining 1/4 teaspoon salt and serve with the Skinny 'Cue Sauce.

Per serving: 217 calories, 2 g fat (0 g saturated, 0 g trans), 4 g protein, 7 g fiber, 22 g sugars, 513 mg sodium, 48 g carbohydrates, 0 mg cholesterol

Mashers never had it this good! I whip mashed spuds into shape for a lean profile that doesn't sacrifice creaminess or flavor. With lots of roasted garlic and tangy, rich low-fat buttermilk, these potatoes totally satisfy my craving for starch. The recipe easily doubles for holiday entertaining. FWB: Garlic

Roasted Garlic and Buttermilk Mashers

SERVES 6

2½ pounds russet (baking) potatoes

1½ teaspoons plus 1 tablespoon sea salt

1 tablespoon extra-virgin olive oil

1 head roasted garlic (below)

¼ cup plus 2 tablespoons buttermilk

 Slim Scoop!

Roasted garlic is a calorie counter's best friend. It spreads "like butta" but doesn't pad your hips like it!

Slice the top third off a large head of garlic, exposing the cloves. Place the head on a square of foil, drizzle with ½ teaspoon of olive oil, and sprinkle with salt and pepper. Wrap the foil around the garlic and roast the bundle at 375°F until the cloves are totally caramelized and soft, about 1 hour.

Halve the potatoes lengthwise and then again crosswise without peeling. Place them in a large pot of water along with 1½ teaspoons of the salt. Cover, bring to a boil, reduce the heat to a gentle boil, and cook until a paring knife easily slips into the centers, about 15 minutes. Drain and set the potatoes aside for 5 minutes.

Heat the olive oil in the same pot over low heat. Return the potatoes to the pan. Squeeze individual cloves out from the head of roasted garlic and mash them into the potatoes. Add the buttermilk and the remaining 1 tablespoon salt. Mash together until the puree is semismooth (it won't be completely smooth because of the potato skins). Serve hot.

Per serving: 194 calories, 8 g fat (1.3 g saturated, 0 g trans), 7 g protein, 5 g fiber, 18 g sugars, 687 mg sodium, 27 g carbohydrates, 0 mg cholesterol

I nominate potatoes as this season's comeback kid. Rustic roasted potatoes are easy and delicious and I eat them all the time. If you're stuck on carb counting, then unstick yourself for just a sec and think about this: Not only are potatoes naturally fat-free, but when you leave the skins on they contain a good amount of fiber and potassium, too.

Simply Obsessed Baked Potatoes

SERVES 6

6 large russet (baking) potatoes

1 tablespoon extra-virgin olive oil

½ teaspoon sea salt

Nonfat plain Greek yogurt (optional)

Chopped scallions or chives (optional)

Preheat the oven to 350°F. Set the potatoes on a rimmed baking sheet and prick them a few times with a fork. Drizzle with the oil, sprinkle with the salt, and rub the potatoes around to make sure they're all slick and seasoned.

Bake until the potatoes are fragrant, the skins are crisp, and a paring knife easily slips into the centers, about 1 hour. Remove from the oven and serve as is or with yogurt and scallions or chives.

Per serving: 313 calories, 2.6 g fat (0.5 g saturated, 0 g trans), 8 g protein, 5 g fiber, 2 g sugars, 150 mg sodium, 67 g carbohydrates, 0 mg cholesterol

♡ Frugal & Fab

I like to roast a few potatoes at once and stow the extras in the fridge for later. They're a wonderful side dish, snack, or a fab main course when loaded with your favorite toppers like sun-dried tomatoes, nonfat Greek yogurt, and chives.

Ⓥ = vegetarian   Ⓥ = vegan

CHAPTER 9

Skinny Sweets & Splurges

Sweets and I go way back.

So you can bet that there is no way anyone is going to deprive me of an occasional naughty treat! The trick is to make them healthier by using ingredients like pear puree or fresh bananas to keep cakes and cookies moist instead of a ton of butter or oil, and by substituting lean ingredients for fatty ones, like almond milk for cream in frostings and fillings. For the times when I truly need a no-holds-barred sugar fix, I make the real thing, and just eat a tiny portion of it. It's always important to know when to say "when." Remember, we want the sweet to be dee-lish on our lips and stay off our sexy hips!

These pretty pink cupcakes don't depend on artificial colors or flavors for their strawberry glow, just real fruit, thank you very much. I use all-fruit strawberry jam and individually quick-frozen strawberries for a wonderful peak berry flavor and soft pinky glow any time of the year. They are a splurge for sure, but worth it. You'll need two pastry bags, a round tip, and a star tip to decorate the cupcakes. FWB: Strawberries

Strawberry Cupcakes

MAKES **12** CUPCAKES

Cupcakes

2 cups cake flour

¾ teaspoon baking soda

¼ teaspoon sea salt

¼ cup buttermilk

¾ teaspoon vanilla extract

3 tablespoons unsalted butter, at room temperature

¾ cup sugar

2 large eggs

1½ cups frozen strawberries, coarsely chopped

Frosting

1½ tablespoons ⅓-less-fat Neufchâtel cream cheese, at room temperature

1½ tablespoons strawberry all-fruit spread

¾ teaspoon fresh lemon juice

7½ cups confectioners' sugar

6 tablespoons unsweetened almond milk

Topping

⅓ cup strawberry all-fruit spread

To make the cupcakes: Preheat the oven to 350°F. Line a 12-cup muffin pan with paper liners. Sift the flour, baking soda, and salt into a medium bowl and set aside. Whisk the buttermilk and vanilla together in a liquid measuring cup and set aside.

Using an electric mixer, cream the butter and sugar together on low speed until combined. Increase the speed to medium-high and beat until very creamy. Add the eggs, one at a time, mixing well and using a rubber spatula to scrape down the bowl between additions. Beat until the mixture is very fluffy. Reduce the speed to medium-low and alternate adding the flour mixture and buttermilk in three additions, starting and ending with the flour mixture, and mixing just until combined. Fold in the strawberries.

Fill the muffin cups three-fourths full with batter. Bake until the cupcakes are domed, resist light pressure, and a toothpick inserted in the center of a cupcake comes out clean, 25 to 30 minutes. Set aside to cool for 10 minutes in the pan, then remove to a wire rack to cool completely.

Meanwhile, to make the frosting: Place the cream cheese in the bowl of a stand mixer. Add the strawberry jam and lemon juice and beat on low speed until combined. Turn off the mixer and sift

(*continued*)

in three-fourths of the confectioners' sugar. Beat on low speed, and once it is nearly combined, gradually add half of the almond milk. Increase the speed to medium-low and beat to lighten the mixture. Turn off the mixer, sift in the remaining confectioners' sugar, beat on low speed, and then pour in the remaining almond milk. Once it is added, increase the mixer speed to medium-high and beat until the frosting is light and airy.

To top the cupcakes: Fill a pastry bag fitted with a plain tip with the ⅓ cup strawberry jam. Push the tip into the center of each cupcake and squeeze a little bit of jam into it. Fit another pastry bag (or clean and dry the first bag) with a star-shaped tip and fill it with the frosting. Squeeze a bit of frosting over the jam mark of each cupcake. The cupcakes can be eaten immediately or kept at room temperature for a few hours before serving. Or refrigerate them overnight and let them stand at room temperature for 20 minutes before serving.

Per cupcake: 499 calories, 5 g fat (2.4 g saturated, 0 g trans), 3 g protein, 1 g fiber, 92 g sugars, 146 mg sodium, 113 g carbohydrates, 44 mg cholesterol

Slim Scoop!
Sometimes fresh isn't best. IQF (individually quick-frozen) fruit is picked at peak ripeness and then flash-frozen to preserve its wonderful flavor, making it a great option for satisfying a blueberry or strawberry craving in the middle of January! Strawberries are a great source of vitamin C, so I like to think that I'm powering up my immune system whenever I bake up a dozen.

These delicious minis are great on-the-go treats or for a midday shot of something sweet and fun. They are bursting with antioxidant-rich blueberries, which tint the babycakes a pretty blue hue; the coconut-lime icing adds a hint of the tropical. They're so small and cute you won't feel guilty for eating these babies—though you may have a bit of an addiction afterward! FWB: Blueberries

Baby Blue Babycakes

MAKES **24** BABYCAKES

Babycakes

2 cups all-purpose flour

2 tablespoons grated lime zest (from 4 limes)

1 teaspoon baking soda

$^1/_4$ teaspoon sea salt

$^1/_2$ cup buttermilk

$^1/_4$ cup nonfat plain Greek yogurt

1 tablespoon fresh lime juice

1 tablespoon vanilla extract

$^1/_4$ cup ($^1/_2$ stick) unsalted butter at room temperature

$^3/_4$ cup sugar

2 large eggs

1 cup frozen blueberries

Icing

1 cup confectioner's sugar

1 tablespoon grated lime zest (from 2 limes)

$1^1/_2$ teaspoons fresh lime juice

1–2 tablespoons unsweetened almond milk or buttermilk

$^3/_4$ cup sweetened flaked coconut

To make the babycakes: Preheat the oven to 350°F. Line the cups of a mini muffin pan with paper liners. Whisk the flour, lime zest, baking soda, and salt together in a large bowl and set aside. Whisk the buttermilk, yogurt, lime juice, and vanilla extract together in a small bowl.

Using an electric mixer, cream the butter and sugar together on low speed until combined. Increase the speed to medium-high and beat until light and fluffy, about 2 minutes. Add the eggs, one at a time, mixing well and using a rubber spatula to scrape down the bowl between additions.

Reduce the speed of the mixer to medium-low and alternate adding the flour mixture and buttermilk mixture in three additions, starting and ending with the flour mixture, and mixing just until combined. Use a rubber spatula to fold in the blueberries until just combined (don't overmix or your batter will turn blue!).

Fill the muffin cups three-fourths full with batter. Bake until the cupcakes are domed and resist light pressure, about 15 minutes. Set aside to cool for 10 minutes in the pan, then remove to a wire rack to cool completely.

To make the icing: Whisk the confectioners' sugar and lime zest together in a small bowl. Add the lime juice and the almond

(*continued*)

milk and whisk until smooth (the consistency should be slightly thicker than melted chocolate). Place the coconut in a shallow bowl. One at a time, dip the babycakes dome-side down in the icing. Once all the babycakes are iced, dip them in the coconut. Let them set up for a few minutes before serving. Store the babycakes at room temperature for up to 1 day.

Per babycake: 124 calories, 3 g fat (2 g saturated, 0 g trans), 2 g protein, 1 g fiber, 13 g sugars, 89 mg sodium, 22 g carbohydrates, 23 mg cholesterol

DIY Icing on the Cake!

Customize your icing to suit your cake and craving! It's easy and much cheaper than buying supersweet, chemical-laden premade frosting in a tub.

The basic recipe is 1 cup of confectioners' sugar whisked with 1½ to 3 tablespoons of almond milk or buttermilk, depending on how thick or thin you want the icing. Use less liquid for an opaque drizzle, more for a transparent glaze.

Blueberry Bundle: Stir ¾ cup fresh or thawed frozen blueberries into the icing.

Cinnamon: Whisk 1 tablespoon ground cinnamon into the confectioners' sugar.

Coconut Dream: Mix 3 cups of sweetened flaked coconut into the icing.

Cream Cheese: Whisk ¾ cup of room temperature Neufchâtel cream cheese with 1 tablespoon of the almond milk or buttermilk. Whisk in the confectioners' sugar and thin out with more liquid if needed.

Double Chocolate: Whisk ⅓ cup unsweetened cocoa powder into the confectioners' sugar and stir in 1½ cups melted semisweet chocolate chips after mixing the almond milk or buttermilk into the sugar.

Limeade: Add 3 tablespoons of lime juice and 1 tablespoon of lime zest to the icing.

Orangesicle: Add 3 tablespoons of orange juice and 1 tablespoon of orange zest to the icing.

Pumpkin Spice: Add 1 tablespoon of pumpkin pie spice to the confectioners' sugar and ⅓ cup of pumpkin puree after whisking the sugar and liquid together.

Raspberry: Add ⅓ cup of raspberry jam or preserves to the icing.

Strawberries and Cream: Add ⅓ cup of strawberry jam or preserves to the icing.

Real lemon juice and zest gives these babycakes their zingy attitude, while a sweet and dreamy lemon curd sends them into overdrive. I love making these cupcakes for birthday parties because when you bite into one, you just can't help but smile, and your friends will too when they realize the time and effort you devoted to making their day special. FWB: Lemon

Lemon Babycakes

MAKES **30** BABYCAKES

Babycakes

3 cups cake flour, sifted

$\frac{1}{4}$ cup grated lemon zest (4–6 lemons)

$\frac{1}{2}$ teaspoon baking soda

$\frac{1}{2}$ teaspoon sea salt

$\frac{1}{2}$ cup buttermilk

$\frac{1}{4}$ cup fresh lemon juice (1–2 lemons)

1 teaspoon vanilla extract

$\frac{1}{2}$ cup (1 stick) unsalted butter, at room temperature

$1\frac{1}{2}$ cups sugar

3 large eggs, at room temperature

Lemon curd

$\frac{1}{2}$ cup fresh lemon juice (2–3 lemons)

$\frac{1}{2}$ cup sugar

$\frac{1}{4}$ cup grated lemon zest (4–6 lemons)

2 large eggs, at room temperature

1 teaspoon vanilla extract

To make the babycakes: Preheat the oven to 325°F. Line the cups of a mini muffin pan with paper liners. Whisk the sifted flour, lemon zest, baking soda, and salt together in a large bowl. Whisk the buttermilk, lemon juice, and vanilla together in a small bowl.

Using an electric mixer, cream the butter and sugar together on low speed until combined. Increase the speed to medium-high and beat until light and fluffy, about 2 minutes. Add the eggs, one at a time, mixing well and using a rubber spatula to scrape down the bowl between additions.

Reduce the speed of the mixer to medium-low and alternate adding the flour mixture and buttermilk mixture in three additions, starting and ending with the flour mixture, and mixing just until combined.

Fill the muffin cups three-fourths full with batter. Bake until the cupcakes are domed and resist light pressure, 18 to 20 minutes. Set aside to cool for 10 minutes in the pan, then remove to a wire rack to cool completely.

Meanwhile, make the lemon curd: Combine the lemon juice and sugar in a small saucepan and bring to a simmer. Add the

(continued)

Icing

5 cups confectioners' sugar

1½ tablespoons ⅓-less-fat Neufchâtel cream cheese, at room temperature

¼ cup unsweetened almond milk

2 tablespoons grated lemon zest (2–3 lemons)

1 tablespoon fresh lemon juice

lemon zest and cook, stirring occasionally, just until the sugar is dissolved, about 2 minutes.

Whisk the eggs together in a medium bowl. Whisk a little of the hot lemon mixture into the eggs to warm them. Once the bottom of the bowl is warm, slowly whisk in the remaining hot lemon mixture. Pour the mixture back into the saucepan and place it over medium-low heat. Cook, stirring constantly, until a few bubbles pop on the surface of the curd and it coats the back of a wooden spoon, 10 to 15 minutes. Remove from the heat immediately and strain the curd through a fine-mesh sieve into a clean bowl. Using a clean whisk or spoon, stir in the vanilla extract. Place a piece of plastic wrap directly on the surface of the curd and cool to room temperature. Chill for at least 30 minutes.

Fill a pastry bag, fitted with a small plain tip, no more than two-thirds full with lemon curd. Twist the top of the bag to close. Press the tip halfway into the center of a babycake and squeeze in a little lemon curd. Lift the tip out and squeeze a little dollop on the top as well. Repeat with the remaining babycakes.

To make the icing: Beat the confectioners' sugar and cream cheese together on low speed until combined (the mixture will be crumbly). Add the almond milk, lemon zest and juice and beat until smooth and creamy. Fill a pastry bag fitted with a star tip, pipe a little swirl of icing on top of each babycake. Serve within 1 hour, or refrigerate the babycakes for up to 1 day and let them stand at room temperature for 20 minutes before serving.

Per babycake: 148 calories, 4 g fat (2 g saturated, 0 g trans), 2 g protein, 0.5 g fiber, 14 g sugars, 66 mg sodium, 26 g carbohydrates, 44 mg cholesterol

Slim Scoop!
Unsweetened almond milk is healthy, creamy, and rich all while adding roughly 40 calories per cup to the profile of a recipe! Sometimes I'm more about health than cash (almond milk is more expensive than regular milk), but it's so delicious that it's worth every penny.

I adore carrot cupcakes and there's no reason to shun them when they're this good for you and delicious! I add more than a cup of grated carrots for extra goodness in each bite, plus crushed pineapple for natural sweetness and moisture. The icing is made in a snap and is so creamy and dreamy, no one will guess it's made with almond milk instead of butter. That little secret is just between you and me! FWB: Carrots

Pineapple-Carrot Cupcakes

MAKES **12** CUPCAKES

Cupcakes

1¼ cups all-purpose flour

1 teaspoon baking soda

½ teaspoon ground cinnamon

½ teaspoon freshly grated nutmeg

¼ teaspoon sea salt

¼ cup vegetable oil

⅓ cup packed dark brown sugar

1 large egg

½ teaspoon vanilla extract

1½ cups grated carrots

½ cup drained canned crushed pineapple

¼ cup walnut pieces (optional)

¼ cup raisins (optional)

Icing

¼ cup ⅓-less-fat Neufchâtel cream cheese, at room temperature

5½ cups confectioners' sugar, sifted

¼ cup unsweetened almond milk

1 teaspoon grated orange zest

1 tablespoon fresh orange juice

1 teaspoon vanilla extract

To make the cupcakes: Preheat the oven to 350°F. Line a 12-cup muffin pan with paper liners. Whisk the flour, baking soda, cinnamon, nutmeg, and salt together in a large bowl and set aside.

Whisk the oil and brown sugar together in a large bowl until combined. Whisk in ¼ cup of water, the egg, and vanilla extract. Stir in the flour mixture until just barely combined. Stir in the carrots, pineapple, walnuts (if desired), and raisins (if desired).

Fill the muffin cups three-fourths full with batter. Bake until the cupcakes are domed, resist light pressure, and a toothpick inserted into the center of a cupcake comes out clean, 15 to 20 minutes. Set aside to cool for 10 minutes in the pan, then remove to a wire rack to cool completely.

To make the icing: Place the cream cheese in the bowl of a stand mixer (or in a large bowl if using a hand mixer) and beat until very light and fluffy. Reduce the speed to low and beat in the confectioners' sugar 1 cup at a time until all of it has been added. Add the almond milk, orange zest, orange juice, and vanilla extract and beat until fluffy. Use a knife (or a pastry bag fitted with a star tip) to frost the cooled cupcakes. Let the icing set up for 10 minutes before serving.

Per cupcake: 361 calories, 6 g fat (1.5 g saturated, 0 g trans), 2 g protein, 1 g fiber, 62 g sugars, 179 mg sodium, 75 g carbohydrates, 21 mg cholesterol

Sometimes, when it comes to chocolate, no substitute will do. That's when I make these decadent, dark, and deeply chocolatey brownies. They're not low-fat or low in calories, but they're so rich that I get my fix from just a small bite. Peppermint candies add a cheap, minty thrill, but if you prefer you can sprinkle ¼ cup walnut pieces over the batter for a different kind of crunch. FWB: Cocoa powder

Dark Chocolate–Peppermint Brownies

MAKES **16** BROWNIES

1 cup semisweet or bittersweet chocolate chips (preferably with a minimum of 65% cacao) or 1 cup chopped bittersweet chocolate

1 cup all-purpose flour

¾ cup unsweetened cocoa powder

½ teaspoon baking soda

Pinch of sea salt

¼ cup (½ stick) unsalted butter, at room temperature

¾ cup packed light or dark brown sugar

2 large eggs

⅓ cup nonfat plain Greek yogurt

½ cup crushed peppermint candies

✔ Slim Scoop!

Dark chocolate can give you a real health and beauty buzz! The cocoa in chocolate encourages our brains to produce mood-boosting serotonin and antioxidant flavonoids that might help reduce blood pressure and cholesterol.

Preheat the oven to 350°F. Lightly coat an 8- or 9-inch square baking pan with cooking spray and set aside.

Place the chocolate in a microwaveable bowl and microwave in 10-second intervals, stirring between each, until the chocolate is melted. Set aside to cool slightly and then scrape it into a large bowl.

Whisk the flour, cocoa powder, baking soda, and salt together in a medium bowl and set aside. Add the butter and brown sugar to the bowl with the melted chocolate and beat with an electric mixer to combine. Beat in the eggs, one at a time, and then add the yogurt. Reduce the speed of the mixer to medium-low and alternate adding the flour mixture and ⅓ cup of water in three additions, starting and ending with the flour mixture, and mixing just until combined.

Using a rubber spatula, scrape the batter into the prepared baking pan. Smooth the surface and then sprinkle the peppermint candies over the top. Bake until the sides are dry and pulling away from the pan and the center resists light pressure, 30 to 40 minutes. Set aside to cool for at least 2 hours, then cut into 16 squares.

Per brownie: 148 calories, 4 g fat (2 g saturated, 0 g trans), 2 g protein, 0.5 g fiber, 14 g sugars, 66 mg sodium, 26 g carbohydrates, 44 mg cholesterol

Maple syrup warms my heart and makes me lick my lips! It adds the most incredible (and natural) sweetness to these wonderfully spicy, moist, and dense dessert bars. With a steamy cup of hazelnut coffee they are just heaven! For an extra coffee kick, substitute 2 tablespoons of strong-brewed coffee or espresso for the almond milk in the glaze. FWB: Walnuts

Maple-Walnut Bars

MAKES **9** BARS

1½ cups all-purpose flour

½ teaspoon ground cinnamon

½ teaspoon freshly grated nutmeg

½ teaspoon baking soda

¼ teaspoon sea salt

1 cup maple syrup

1 teaspoon vanilla extract

¼ cup (½ stick) unsalted butter, at room temperature

⅓ cup packed dark or light brown sugar

2 large eggs, lightly beaten

½ cup quick oats

¾ cup chopped walnuts

¾ cup confectioners' sugar

2 tablespoons unsweetened almond milk

Preheat the oven to 350°F. Lightly coat an 8-inch square baking pan with cooking spray.

Whisk the flour, cinnamon, nutmeg, baking soda, and salt together in a medium bowl and set aside. Stir the maple syrup and vanilla together in a small bowl.

Using an electric mixer, beat the butter and brown sugar together on low speed until combined. Increase the speed to medium-high and beat until creamy, about 2 minutes. Add the eggs, one at a time, scraping the bowl between additions. Alternate adding the flour mixture with the maple mixture, starting and ending with the flour mixture, mixing on low speed until well combined. Use a wooden spoon to stir in the oats and nuts.

Scrape the mixture into the prepared baking pan and smooth the top. Bake until the center resists light pressure, 40 to 45 minutes. Place the pan on a wire rack to cool completely.

While the cake cools, make the icing. Sift the confectioners' sugar into a medium bowl and whisk in the almond milk until the icing is smooth. Run a knife around the edges of the pan, invert the cake onto a plate. Drizzle the icing over the cooled cake and let it set for at least 10 minutes before cutting into 9 bars.

Per bar: 384 calories, 13 g fat (4 g saturated, 0 g trans), 6 g protein, 2 g fiber, 40 g sugars, 139 mg sodium, 63 g carbohydrates, 61 mg cholesterol

I love syrah for poaching pears—it's dry and not too sweet. The spices, citrus zest, and sugar really make this a fantastic treat—it's like the pears are taking a hot, sexy vino bath! When I can find Meyer lemons in the wintertime, I like to grate some zest over the sorbet. You can serve the pears whole, but I prefer to halve them to serve more people (with fewer calories per serving). FWB: Red wine

Bosc Pears in Mulled Vino

SERVES 4 TO 8

1 bottle (750 ml) syrah wine (preferably Californian)

1 cup sugar

2 cinnamon sticks

1 whole star anise

5 whole cloves

1 strip lemon zest, 4 inches long and ¼ inch wide

4 strips orange zest, 4 inches long and ¼ inch wide

1 vanilla bean or 1 teaspoon vanilla extract

4 Bosc pears, peeled, stem on

1 pint lemon sorbet

Combine the wine with 2 cups of water in a large saucepan and bring to a simmer. Add the sugar, cinnamon, star anise, cloves, citrus zests, and vanilla, and simmer, stirring occasionally, until the sugar is dissolved, about 2 minutes.

Add the pears, reduce the heat to low, cover, and cook gently until the pears are stained a deep, dark purple color, about 30 minutes; turn the pears once or twice while they poach. Turn off the heat, uncover the pan, and let the pears cool in the cooking liquid.

Remove the pears from the saucepan and set aside. Strain the liquid through a sieve and discard the spices. Pour the liquid back into the pan and bring to a simmer over medium-high heat. Reduce the heat to medium-low and simmer until it is syrupy and reduced by half, 45 to 50 minutes. Taste and add more sugar if needed. Cool the syrup to room temperature.

Place the pears on a work surface. Halve them lengthwise and core them using a melon baller. Place a pear half in a bowl, top with a scoop of sorbet, and drizzle with the syrah syrup. Serve the warm vino in espresso cups as a complementary beverage if you like.

Per ½ pear: 265 calories, 0 g fat (0 g saturated, 0 g trans), 0 g protein, 2 g fiber, 44 g sugars, 21 mg sodium, 50 g carbohydrates, 0 mg cholesterol

As if steamy apples perfumed with cinnamon and nutmeg served hot-from-the-oven in cute little mugs weren't fabulous enough, this is low in fat, too! You save major calories and fat grams by losing the piecrust and topping the mugs with a flakey phyllo crust instead. I like to prep them ahead of time and pop them in the oven right when we sit down for dinner. By the time the last bite is gone, hot apple mugs are ready to be served! FWB: Apples

Mom's Apple Mug Pie

SERVES 4

2 tablespoons unsalted butter

8 large Golden Delicious or Fuji apples, halved and sliced ¼ inch thick

½ cup sugar

1 tablespoon ground cinnamon

½ teaspoon freshly grated nutmeg

Salt

2 tablespoons fresh lemon juice

2 tablespoons all-purpose flour plus extra for rolling

½ cup dried cranberries (optional)

1 large egg

5 sheets phyllo dough

Preheat the oven to 350°F. Melt the butter in a large skillet over medium heat. Add the apples, sugar, cinnamon, nutmeg, and a pinch of salt, toss to combine, and gently cook, stirring occasionally, until the apples are golden and soft, about 15 minutes.

Add the lemon juice and then sprinkle in the flour, gently stirring it into the apples (if the pan seems dry, stir in 1 to 2 tablespoons of water). Be sure to scrape all the good browned stuff up off the bottom of the pan. Stir in the dried cranberries (if desired), turn off the heat, and divide the apples among four 8-ounce or six 6-ounce mugs or ramekins.

Whisk the egg, a pinch of salt, and 1 teaspoon of water together. Place a sheet of phyllo on a work surface. Spray lightly with cooking spray. Top with 4 more sheets, spraying each lightly. Use a sharp knife to cut out 4 or 6 squares. Keep the phyllo covered with a slightly damp paper towel to prevent it from drying out as you work. Brush a little egg wash onto the rim of each mug and cover with a phyllo stack. Lightly brush the pastry with a little more egg wash. Place the mugs on a rimmed baking sheet and bake until the crust is golden brown, about 20 minutes. Serve warm or at room temperature.

Per serving: 418 calories, 9 g fat (4.5 g saturated, 0 g trans), 5 g protein, 8 g fiber, 61 g sugars, 218 mg sodium, 88 g carbohydrates, 68 mg cholesterol

These absolutely delicious baked apples were one of my favorites as a kid. They were a "throw and go" dessert that my mom always put in the oven just before dinner. By the time the table was cleared, they were done and the house smelled amazing. Now that I'm all grown up, I make these as an elegant finish to any dinner party, because simple is always elegant. FWB: Apples

Baked Cinnamon-Sugar Apples

SERVES 6

¾ cup sliced almonds

¼ cup granulated sugar

¼ cup packed light or dark brown sugar

½ cup dried cranberries (optional)

2 teaspoons ground cinnamon

¼ teaspoon freshly grated nutmeg

6 Red Delicious or Fuji apples

Cinnamon sugar for serving (optional)

Preheat the oven to 350°F. Place the almonds in a medium skillet and gently toast over medium heat, shaking the pan often, until they're browned, 2 to 4 minutes. Transfer to a small plate to cool and then place them in a small bowl. Add the sugars, cranberries (if desired), cinnamon, and nutmeg to the almonds and toss gently to combine.

Set the apples on a cutting board. Cut a small slice off of the bottom of each so they stand upright without wobbling. Using a paring knife, core the apples through the stem end, but do not go all the way through (so you remove about three-fourths of the core, leaving the bottom intact). Use a vegetable peeler to remove about 1 inch of peel from the top of each apple.

Place the apples in a 9 × 13-inch glass baking dish and fill the cored centers with the sugared almonds. After filling the cores, if you have leftover sugared almonds, just sprinkle them over the apples. Bake until the apples feel soft when pressed lightly and they are golden where they were peeled, 50 minutes to 1 hour. Set aside to cool slightly. Add a few tablespoons of water to the juices in the baking dish to make it pourable. Place the apples in bowls, drizzle the syrup over the top, and serve sprinkled with more cinnamon sugar, if desired.

Per serving: 231 calories, 6 g fat (0.5 g saturated, 0 g trans), 3 g protein, 6 g fiber, 37 g sugars, 5 mg sodium, 46 g carbohydrates, 0 mg cholesterol

This is a beaut of a pie because it tastes so naughty, but she's really a good girl in disguise, thanks to lean silken tofu and almond milk! Just like Louboutin heels, there's no substitute for the real thing, so for the best flavor and silky texture, buy the best chocolate chips you can find. FWB: Tofu, cocoa powder

Chocolate Silk Pie

SERVES **8**

Crust

1½ cups graham cracker crumbs

1 tablespoon sugar

½ teaspoon ground cinnamon

2 tablespoons unsweetened almond milk

Filling

1 cup semisweet chocolate chips or chopped semisweet chocolate

1 package (14 ounces) silken tofu

¼ cup unsweetened almond milk

2 tablespoons unsweetened cocoa powder

2 tablespoons sugar

Slim Scoop!

Using silken tofu instead of heavy cream slashes 50 percent of the calories and fat from this, and ups the protein content, too.

To make the crust: Preheat the oven to 350°F. Place the graham cracker crumbs in a large mixing bowl and stir in the sugar and cinnamon. Add the almond milk and toss with a fork until the mixture looks like wet sand. Press the crumbs firmly into a 9-inch pie plate. Bake the crust until it is dry looking, about 10 minutes. Remove from the oven and set aside to cool. Leave the oven on.

Meanwhile, make the filling: Place the chocolate in a microwave-able bowl and microwave in 10-second intervals, stirring between each, until the chocolate is melted. Set aside to cool slightly and then scrape it into a large bowl. (You can also melt the chocolate in a large bowl over a pan with 1 inch of barely simmering water, stirring the chocolate occasionally, until it is completely melted.)

Place the tofu, almond milk, cocoa, and sugar in a food processor. Drizzle the melted chocolate over the top and process until very smooth. Pour onto the cooled crust and bake until the filling is set and jiggles only slightly in the very center when tapped, about 25 minutes. Cool on a wire rack for 2 hours, then cover loosely with plastic wrap and refrigerate overnight (or for at least 8 hours) before serving.

Per serving: 213 calories, 9 g fat (4 g saturated, 0 g trans), 4 g protein, 3 g fiber, 21 g sugars, 106 mg sodium, 32 g carbohydrates, 0 mg cholesterol

Homemade Chocolate–Peanut Butter Crunch Cups

MAKES **20** PEANUT BUTTER CUPS

1 bag (12 ounces) semisweet or bittersweet chocolate chips

20 mini cupcake liners

1 tablespoon unsalted butter

¾ cup creamy natural peanut butter

¼ cup confectioners' sugar

1 cup crispy rice cereal

Place the chocolate in a microwaveable bowl and microwave in 10-second intervals, stirring between each, until the chocolate is melted. Set aside to cool slightly and then scrape it into a large bowl. (You can also melt the chocolate in a large bowl over a pan with 1 inch of barely simmering water, stirring the chocolate occasionally, until it is completely melted.)

Using a small paint brush or pastry brush, coat the bottoms and three-fourths of the way up the sides of the cupcake liners with some of the chocolate (set aside the rest for later). The coating should be fairly thick so that when the liners are peeled off, the chocolate shell doesn't crack. Place the coated liners on a plate and refrigerate for at least 20 minutes or up to several hours.

While the shells chill, make the peanut butter filling. Melt the butter in a medium saucepan over medium heat. Stir in the peanut butter using a wooden spoon and then add the confectioners' sugar and rice cereal. Mix until well combined and gooey looking (it should look like slightly melted chunky peanut butter). Allow the mixture to cool slightly; 10 to 15 minutes should do it (if the mixture is too hot, it will melt the chocolate shells).

(*continued*)

Remove the chocolate cups from the refrigerator. Use a teaspoon to fill each shell three-fourths full with peanut butter filling (you can use a wet finger or the back of a spoon to smooth out the top if you like). If the remaining chocolate in the bowl has hardened, re-melt it in the microwave in 5-second bursts. Spoon some chocolate over the peanut butter filling, spreading and turning the shell so the chocolate seals the cup. Return to the refrigerator for at least 20 minutes (or up to 2 weeks in an airtight plastic container) to harden. Serve chilled.

Per peanut butter cup: 158 calories, 11 g fat (4 g saturated, 0 g trans), 3 g protein, 2 g fiber, 11 g sugars, 49 mg sodium, 16 g carbohydrates, 2 mg cholesterol

Chocolate, the Ultimate FWB!

I'm often asked if I eat chocolate. Um, are you messing with me? I have something to satisfy my choco craving—whether it's a handful of dark chocolate–covered almonds or a piece of high-quality, 70 percent cacao chocolate bar—almost every single day! As with everything, moderation is key; but deprive yourself entirely and you'll go nutzo. Besides, chocolate is actually a FWB! Here's why:

Flavonoids. Chocolate has been shown to contain antiaging antioxidants called flavonoids, the same antioxidants found in blueberries and raspberries. These compounds fight free radicals to keep you looking fabulous and youthful! They also can help keep cholesterol in check, reducing the risk of blood clots and clogged arteries.

Endorphins and more. Chocolate causes the brain to release endorphins, your body's all-natural feel-good buzz; phenylethylamine, which is associated with the feeling of falling in love; and anandamide, an all-natural high!

And remember, when it comes to chocolate, the darker the better. Dark chocolate contains more cacao and more antioxidants—personally, I don't mess with chocolate unless it's at least 70 percent cacao.

Hello bonbon makeover! These amazing bites of heaven are filled with healthy chunks of banana rather than ice cream for a creamy and lusciously low-fat bite. I make them when I need a quick chocolate fix. For an even lighter version, skip the nuts. FWB: Bananas

Chocolate-Banana Bonbons

MAKES ABOUT **32** BONBONS

1 bag (12 ounces) semisweet chocolate chips

¼ cup slivered almonds

¼ cup chopped walnuts

¼ cup sweetened shredded coconut

1 tablespoon canola oil

4 medium semiripe bananas, cut into ¾-inch pieces

Sprinkles, crushed pistachios, chopped pecans, or other toppings of your choice (optional)

Place the chocolate in a microwaveable bowl and microwave in 10-second intervals, stirring between each, until the chocolate is melted. Set aside to cool slightly and then scrape it into a large bowl. (You can also melt the chocolate in a large bowl over a pan with 1 inch of barely simmering water, stirring the chocolate occasionally, until it is completely melted.)

Line a baking sheet with parchment paper. Place the almonds, walnuts, and coconut in separate bowls. Stir the oil into the chocolate and set it aside for 2 minutes. Add a few bananas to the chocolate and stir with a fork to make sure they're completely coated. Carefully roll or dip each banana slice in the topping(s) of your choice. Place them on the baking sheet and freeze for at least 1 hour and up to overnight. Serve cold.

Per bonbon: 82 calories, 5 g fat (2 g saturated, 0 g trans), 1 g protein, 1 g fiber, 8 g sugars, 3 mg sodium, 11 g carbohydrates, 0 mg cholesterol

If you can make a smoothie, you can make sorbet, and you don't even need an expensive ice cream machine to do it—just a little bit of time, a whisk, and a freezer! The best part is that you can indulge in this peach sorbet any time of year because it's made with inexpensive frozen peaches. The raspberries give it a to-die-for color, but they are not a must. Topped with some fresh berries, this is a perfect ending to any meal.

Creamy Peach Sorbet

SERVES **4**

½ cup sugar

4 cups frozen peaches

½ cup frozen raspberries (optional)

¼ cup fresh lemon juice

Combine the sugar and 1 cup of water in a small saucepan over low heat. Stir until the sugar is dissolved, 1 to 2 minutes. Increase the heat to medium-high and bring to a strong simmer. Simmer for 1 minute, then set aside to cool. Refrigerate the syrup to chill thoroughly before making the sorbet.

Place the peaches, raspberries (if desired), and lemon juice in a blender along with the chilled sugar syrup. Puree until the mixture is completely smooth, then pour it into a medium metal bowl. Freeze for 1 hour.

Remove from the freezer and whisk the mixture to smooth it out. Return to the freezer for 1 hour, then whisk again to combine. Repeat 2 or 3 more times until the sorbet is completely frozen and not at all liquidy, about 4 to 5 hours in total. Before serving, let the sorbet sit at room temperature for 5 to 10 minutes (depending on how warm or cold your kitchen is) before scooping.

Per serving: 161 calories, 0 g fat (0 g saturated, 0 g trans), 1 g protein, 1 g fiber, 38 g sugars, 0 mg sodium, 41 g carbohydrates, 0 mg cholesterol

Yep, you can wear your miniskirt and eat dessert—even cheesecake! The secret is silken tofu to keep you slim and trim and keep the cheesecake creamy. Strawberries add sweetness and flavor that I think is the best with cheesecake. See? You can have it all! FWB: Tofu

Sexy Strawberry Cheesecake

SERVES **6**

Crust

1½ cups graham cracker crumbs

1 tablespoon sugar

½ teaspoon ground cinnamon

2 tablespoons unsweetened almond milk

Filling

10 ounces silken tofu

8 ounces ⅓-less-fat Neufchâtel cream cheese, at room temperature

½ cup sugar

½ cup frozen strawberries, partially thawed

6 large fresh strawberries, thinly sliced

To make the crust: preheat the oven to 350°F. Combine the graham cracker crumbs, sugar, and cinnamon in a large mixing bowl. Add the almond milk and toss with a fork to combine until the mixture looks like wet sand. Press the crumbs into a 9-inch pie plate, making an even layer across the bottom, using your fingers or the bottom of a measuring cup to make the crumbs smooth and packed. Bake the crust until it is dry looking, about 10 minutes. Cool on a wire rack. Leave the oven on.

To make the filling: Place the tofu in a food processor and process until smooth. Add the cream cheese and sugar and process until the mixture is creamy. Add the frozen strawberries and process until the mixture is completely smooth.

Pour the filling into the pie crust and bake until the filling is set, about 30 minutes. Cool completely on a wire rack. Cover with plastic wrap and refrigerate for at least 2 hours or overnight before serving with the fresh strawberries.

Per serving: 289 calories, 11 g fat (6 g saturated, 0 g trans), 8 g protein, 1 g fiber, 28 g sugars, 293 mg sodium, 39 g carbohydrates, 27 mg cholesterol

A mug of coffee and a wedge of this super moist coffee cake makes for a wonderfully chill Sunday morning without all of the sugar and fat (or worse yet, the shortening you'd get in a packaged cake). The secret ingredient in this beautifully natural coffee cake is pear baby food! I like to bake the cake in a heart-shaped cake pan, but any 10-cup pan will do.

Maple Heart Coffee Cake

SERVES 12

Cake

3¾ cups all-purpose flour

1 teaspoon baking soda

1 teaspoon ground cinnamon

1 teaspoon salt

1½ cups buttermilk

1 jar (4 ounces) pear baby food

2 tablespoons strong brewed coffee or espresso

¼ cup (½ stick) unsalted butter, at room temperature

¾ cup packed light or dark brown sugar

½ cup maple syrup

2 large eggs

Glaze

1 cup confectioners' sugar

⅛ teaspoon ground cinnamon

2 tablespoons maple syrup

1 tablespoon unsweetened almond milk or buttermilk

To make the cake: Preheat the oven to 350°F. Lightly coat a 12-cup Bundt pan (or a 10-cup heart-shaped cake pan) with cooking spray and set aside. Whisk the flour, baking soda, cinnamon, and salt together in a large bowl and set aside. Whisk the buttermilk, baby food, and coffee together in a medium bowl.

Using an electric mixer, beat the butter, brown sugar, and maple syrup together on low speed until combined. Increase the speed to medium-high and beat until light and fluffy, about 2 minutes. Beat in the eggs, one at a time.

Increase the mixer speed to low and alternate adding the flour mixture and buttermilk mixture in three additions, starting and ending with the flour mixture, and mixing just until combined. Scrape the batter into the pan and bake until the cake is golden brown and a toothpick inserted into the center comes out clean, 45 to 50 minutes. Set the pan on a wire rack to cool for 30 minutes, then turn the cake out onto a platter.

To make the glaze: Whisk the confectioners' sugar and cinnamon together in a medium bowl. Add the maple syrup and almond milk and whisk until smooth. Drizzle the cake with the glaze. Allow the glaze to set for about 10 minutes before serving.

Per serving: 343 calories, 5 g fat (3 g saturated, 0 g trans), 6 g protein, 1 g fiber, 36 g sugars, 351 mg sodium, 68 g carbohydrates, 47 mg cholesterol

I'm totally bananas for these gooey, soft, and super tasty chocolate chip cookies. The bananas keep them soft and give them a nice potassium and B_6 boost, while the oats add all that fiber goodness. The chocolate? Well that's great for smiles and that so-important "mmmm" factor. FWB: Oats

Gone Bananas Chocolate Chip–Oat Cookies

MAKES **2** DOZEN COOKIES

¾ cup all-purpose flour

1 teaspoon ground cinnamon

½ teaspoon baking soda

¼ teaspoon sea salt

2 tablespoons unsalted butter, at room temperature

1 cup packed light brown sugar

1 large egg

1 teaspoon vanilla extract

½ cup mashed banana (1 small or ½ large banana)

2 cups quick oats

1 cup semisweet chocolate chips

Slim Scoop!

Bananas add moisture and tenderness to low-fat cookies, cakes, and cupcakes. Next time you have a slightly overripe one, place it in a resealable freezer bag and save it for your next batch of low-fat cookies. You'll be so glad you did.

Preheat the oven to 350°F. Whisk the flour, cinnamon, baking soda, and salt together in a medium bowl and set aside.

Using an electric mixer, cream the butter and brown sugar together on medium speed until creamy, 1 to 1½ minutes. Add the egg and vanilla extract and beat to combine. Mix in the mashed banana and ¼ cup of water, beating until incorporated. Add the flour mixture and beat on low speed until just combined. Add the oats and chocolate chips and mix briefly. Chill the cookie dough in the refrigerator for 15 minutes.

Line a rimmed baking sheet with foil and coat lightly with cooking spray. Use a tablespoon to scoop out 1½-inch dough balls, placing them about 1 inch apart on the baking sheet. Bake until just golden on top, about 10 minutes. Cool on the sheet for 10 minutes before transferring to a wire rack to cool completely.

Per cookie: 127 calories, 4 g fat (2 g saturated, 0 g trans), 2 g protein, 1 g fiber, 14 g sugars, 49 mg sodium, 22 g carbohydrates, 11 mg cholesterol

These tender cookies are a great fall treat. They offer a double dose of yummy vitamin A-packed pumpkin flavor— first in the cookie (it's the pumpkin puree that keeps these babies so soft) and then in the pumpkin icing. With cinnamon, nutmeg, pumpkin, and brown sugar, the fragrance of these cookies baking is like fall aromatherapy that fills your home with warmth and love. FWB: Pumpkin

Spiced Pumpkin Cookies

MAKES **2** DOZEN COOKIES

Cookies

2 cups all-purpose flour

2 teaspoons ground cinnamon

1 teaspoon baking powder

$^1/_2$ teaspoon baking soda

$^1/_2$ teaspoon freshly grated nutmeg

$^1/_2$ teaspoon sea salt

$^3/_4$ cup packed light brown sugar

$^1/_4$ cup ($^1/_2$ stick) unsalted butter, at room temperature

$^3/_4$ cup canned unsweetened pumpkin puree

1 large egg

1 teaspoon vanilla extract

Icing

2 cups confectioners' sugar

1 tablespoon unsalted butter, melted

1 tablespoon canned unsweetened pumpkin puree

1 teaspoon vanilla extract

1 teaspoon ground cinnamon

1–2 tablespoons unsweetened almond milk

To make the cookies: Preheat the oven to 350°F. Whisk the flour, cinnamon, baking powder, baking soda, nutmeg, and salt together in a medium bowl and set aside.

Using an electric mixer, beat the brown sugar and butter together on medium speed until light and creamy, 1 to 1$^1/_2$ minutes. Add the pumpkin, egg, and vanilla extract and beat to combine. Add the flour mixture and beat on low speed until just combined. Chill the cookie dough for 15 minutes.

Line a rimmed baking sheet with parchment paper. Use a tablespoon to scoop out the cookie batter and roll it between your palms into 1$^1/_2$-inch balls. Place them on the baking sheet leaving about 1 inch between cookies. Flatten the balls slightly and bake until the edges are firm and the center is still soft, about 15 minutes. Cool the cookies on the pan for 10 minutes, then transfer to a wire rack to cool completely.

To make the icing: Sift the confectioners' sugar into a medium bowl. Add the melted butter, pumpkin puree, vanilla extract, cinnamon, and almond milk. Whisk together until completely smooth. Drizzle the glaze over the cookies. Let the icing harden for at least 10 minutes before serving.

Per cookie: 132 calories, 3 g fat (2 g saturated, 0 g trans), 1 g protein, 1 g fiber, 17 g sugars, 82 mg sodium, 26 g carbohydrates, 15 mg cholesterol

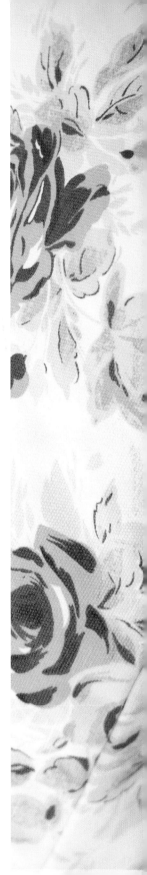

CHAPTER 10

The Pampered Pantry

Want to save some serious dinero on making yourself glowing and gorgeous? Then make your own beauty products! You could also share the wealth and the savings: Double, triple, or quadruple the recipes in this section and invite your girlfriends over for a delicious "pampered pantry" night of at-home spa treatments and homemade mini bites (pages 30–57). If you have oranges, brown sugar, avocados, pineapples, bananas, oats, olive oil, or even cocoa (yes, chocolate!) on hand, then you can make some fabulous treatments for skin, hair, and nails. Major bonus besides the low price tag: no chemicals or other bogus ingredients, just all-natural, good stuff for a most beautiful you!

For Best Results, Test First

We all have different skin types and some of us are more sensitive or prone to irritation than others. Because we all react differently to various ingredients, be sure to test a bit of the beauty treatment on your inner arm before using. If any kind of allergic reaction occurs, rinse off immediately. In addition, try to buy organic ingredients if you plan on using them for beauty treatments. Your skin might have an adverse reaction to the residues from pesticides or other chemicals.

MOISTURIZING OLIVE OIL: There are almost infinite ways to use my extra-virgin friend to stay beautiful inside and out.

Conditioning Shine: Rub 1 teaspoon of extra-virgin olive oil into dry, clean hair (especially those ends!). Wrap your hair in a warm, damp towel and let the oil penetrate for up to 20 minutes before rinsing with warm water.

De-Frizz: Place a drop or two in your palm, rub between your hands, and gloss over dry hair.

Eye Makeup Remover and Moisturizer: My sis taught me this great trick! Dab a few drops on a cotton ball and use to gently wipe off eye makeup.

Foot Rub: Before you go to bed, rub a few drops into your feet, making sure to get those rough areas. Put on cozy socks and in the morning, wake up to softer, moisturized feet.

Nail Treatment: Dip a cotton swab in olive oil and rub it into your cuticles, then buff onto clean nails for a nice shine.

Bath Soak: Add a few drops to a warm bath.

Moisturizer: Rub a little onto rough elbows, knees, or any area that needs a little bit of TLC.

EXFOLIATING BROWN SUGAR: A cheap and easy way to exfoliate skin, getting rid of dullness and getting on a gorgeous glow. For best results, exfoliate at least once a month (depending on your skin type).

Sugar and Spice Rub: Mix ½ cup brown sugar with 2 tablespoons extra-virgin olive oil, 2 teaspoons quick oats, ½ teaspoon ground cinnamon, and

$^1/_2$ teaspoon freshly grated nutmeg in a small bowl. Apply to your skin in a circular motion in the shower and rinse off.

Take Me to Maui Sugar Scrub: Place $^1/_4$ cup guava or mango chunks in a food processor and process until smooth (or mash in a small bowl with a fork). Scrape into a small bowl and stir in $^1/_4$ cup brown sugar, 1 tablespoon coconut milk, and 1$^1/_2$ teaspoons extra-virgin olive oil. Apply to your skin in a circular motion in the shower and rinse off.

SOOTHING OATS: Oats are a great skin treatment ingredient that help to calm sensitive skin and condition oily skin without making it greasy. Who knew Quaker could be so sexy?

Comforting Oat Face Wash: Mix 2 tablespoons quick oats (or old-fashioned rolled oats pulsed in a food processor) with 1 tablespoon plain yogurt and $^1/_2$ teaspoon honey. Gently massage over your face (avoiding eye area). Rinse well.

Rejuvenating Oat and Sugar Scrub: Mix 1 tablespoon quick oats, 1 teaspoon brown sugar, 1 teaspoon soymilk, and a pinch of freshly grated nutmeg in a small bowl. Gently rub onto your face (avoiding eye area) and rinse well. (Quadruple for a whole-body treatment!)

Oatmeal and Banana Moisturizing Mask: Mash one-quarter of a ripe banana in a small bowl and mix in 2 tablespoons quick oats, 1 teaspoon almond milk or soymilk, and a pinch of freshly grated nutmeg or ground cinnamon. Pat onto your face (avoiding eye area) and leave on for 5 to 10 minutes before rinsing off with warm water.

Soothing Honey-Oat Milk Bath: Mix 2 tablespoons quick oats, 1 tablespoon almond milk or soymilk, and $^1/_2$ tablespoon honey in a small bowl. Snip off the foot and lower leg portion of an old (clean!) pair of panty hose. Put the honey-oat mixture into the foot, tie shut, and place in the tub under warm running water. (Or place the mixture into a cheesecloth or muslin sachet and knot shut.)

PAMPERING PINEAPPLE: Pineapple contains a natural anti-inflammatory enzyme, called bromelain, that is great for the skin and helps reduce swelling and puffiness.

Soothing Crushed Pineapple Mask: Blend 2 tablespoons drained canned crushed pineapple with 2 teaspoons quick oats and 1½ teaspoons honey. Pat onto your face (avoiding the eye area) and leave on for 20 minutes. Rinse well.

Tropical Crushed Pineapple and Coconut Scrub: Mix 2 tablespoons drained canned crushed pineapple with 2 tablespoons shredded coconut and 1½ teaspoons turbinado sugar (a.k.a. Sugar in the Raw—grab a few extra sugar packets next time you get a to-go coffee!) in a small bowl. Rub onto your skin in circular motions while in the shower. Rinse well.

GO BANANAS: Who doesn't have an overripe banana hanging around from time to time? Besides their rich and creamy texture, they have lots of antioxidants to refresh tired skin. Keep ripe bananas in the freezer and defrost whenever you need a quick beauty fix.

Bananarama Mask: Mash one-quarter of a ripe banana in a bowl (if you have oily skin, add 1 tablespoon quick oats). Apply to your face (avoiding the eye area) and leave on for 10 minutes before rinsing.

Banana-Honey Mask: Mash one-quarter of a ripe banana in a small bowl. Mix in 1 tablespoon egg white, 1 teaspoon honey, and ½ teaspoon extra-virgin olive oil. Apply to your face (avoiding the eye area) and leave on for 10 minutes before gently wiping off with a warm washcloth.

COMFORTING CINNAMON: So comforting and warm, cinnamon might be my favorite spice of all. It contains antibacterial and antifungal properties as well as a natural grittiness that helps cleanse the skin—great for battling emergency breakouts and flare-ups. Cinnamon can cause irritation, so be sure to try the treatments out on your inner arm before applying to your face.

Cinnie-Orange Face Scrub: Mix 1 tablespoon brown sugar with 1½ teaspoons extra-virgin olive oil, 1½ teaspoons freshly grated orange zest, and ¼ teaspoon ground cinnamon in a small bowl. Gently smooth the mixture onto your face (avoiding the eye area); you might feel a mild tingling sensation, which is totally normal—if it's at all uncomfortable, rinse immediately. Rinse off with warm water and a washcloth.

Cinnamon-Ginger Body Scrub: Mix ¼ cup brown sugar with 1 tablespoon extra-virgin olive oil, 1 teaspoon ground cinnamon, and 1 teaspoon grated fresh ginger in a small bowl. Apply to your skin in circular motions in the shower and rinse.

EXCEPTIONAL EGGS: Tightening, conditioning, and glossing, eggs are great for your skin and hair. The egg whites are like natural botox for your face, while the yolks offer great deep conditioning for tresses.

Protein Power Egg White and Oat Mask: Whisk together 1 egg white and ¼ cup quick oats. Pat onto your face and leave it on for 15 minutes (you'll feel a tightening effect). Rinse with warm water and a washcloth.

Egg White and Honey Mask: Whisk together 1 tablespoon egg white and 1½ teaspoons honey. Pat onto your face and let it set up for 15 minutes (you'll feel a tightening effect). Rinse with warm water and a washcloth.

Smooth Mane Serum: Whip 2 egg yolks and 1 tablespoon white vinegar until foamy in a small bowl. While in the shower, tilt your head back and pour the mixture over your hair, massaging it in. Let it penetrate for 5 minutes before rinsing. Do this once a month for smooth, gorgeous hair.

Conditioning Yogi Yolk Serum: Whisk 1 egg yolk with 1 tablespoon plain yogurt in a small bowl. While in the shower, massage into hair and let it penetrate for 15 to 20 minutes before rinsing.

Yolk and Avocado Major Hair Drench: Whisk 1 egg yolk, 1 teaspoon extra-virgin olive oil, and 1 teaspoon honey together in a small bowl. Using a fork, mash in one-half of an avocado. While in the shower, apply the paste first to your ends and then all over your hair. Let penetrate for 15 to 20 minutes before rinsing.

Sweet and Silky Hair Mask: Whisk 1 egg yolk with 1 tablespoon plain yogurt, 1 tablespoon honey, and ½ teaspoon extra-virgin olive oil in a small bowl until it makes a sudsy paste. Apply the paste to your hair and then wrap in a towel. Let the mask penetrate for 20 minutes before rinsing.

FIRMING YOGURT: Amazing for the body, inside and out! Lactic acid moisturizes, tightens, and nourishes skin.

Yogurt-Honey Mask: Whisk 1 tablespoon plain yogurt with 1 teaspoon honey in a small bowl. Apply to face and leave on for 20 minutes before gently removing with a warm washcloth.

Major Moisture Mask: Mash one-quarter of a ripe avocado in a bowl and stir in 1 tablespoon plain yogurt. Apply to face and leave on for 10 minutes before gently removing with a warm washcloth.

SUPERDUPER AVOCADOS: Soothing and rich, avocados are great for your skin and hair. Buy them when they're on sale and treat yourself!

Sweet Avo-Honey Mask: Use a fork to mash one-quarter of an avocado in a small bowl. Stir in 2 teaspoons honey and apply to your face. After 10 minutes, rinse off with warm water.

20-Minute Miracle Mask: Use a fork to mash one-quarter of an avocado in a small bowl. Stir in 1 tablespoon egg white and $\frac{1}{2}$ teaspoon extra-virgin olive oil, mixing until very creamy. Apply to your face and rinse off after 10 minutes.

Ultimate Avocado Hair Mask: Use a fork to mash one-half of an avocado in a small bowl. Whisk in 1 egg yolk and 1 teaspoon extra-virgin olive oil. Work into dry hair, starting midway from your scalp and working your way down to the ends. Wrap in a towel and let it penetrate for 30 minutes before rinsing.

CHOCOHOLIC TREATMENTS: Chocolate without the calories! Amino acids rejuvenate skin while the delicious smell lifts your mood.

Chocolate Obsession Mask: Whisk $1\frac{1}{2}$ teaspoons unsweetened cocoa powder, $1\frac{1}{2}$ teaspoons honey, $\frac{3}{4}$ teaspoon plain yogurt, and $\frac{1}{2}$ teaspoon quick oats in a small bowl. Apply to your face (avoiding the eye area) and leave on for 15 to 20 minutes before gently removing with a warm washcloth.

My Favorite Things Mask: People always ask me what my favorite foods are, and the answer is easy—avocados and chocolate! But I never put them together . . . until now! Use a fork to mash one-quarter of an avocado in a small bowl. Mix in $1\frac{1}{2}$ teaspoons unsweetened cocoa powder to make a smooth paste. Apply to your face (avoiding the eye area) and leave on for 20 minutes before gently removing with a warm washcloth.

Acknowledgments

Mom, you're my inspiration and I am forever grateful for you; I love you, Okasan! Dad, you're the kind of guy that every woman should marry. You taught me always to give 150 percent. Love you more than you will ever know. Sis, you're the most philanthropic individual I know. Thank you for being my sister and my friend. I love you.

Miss Pam Krauss, my ichiban editor, you're absolutely brilliant, talented, and stunning—my #1 mentor and inspiration! The incredibly talented Quentin Bacon, thank you for such stunning photos; the images clearly speak for themselves. Big THANK YOU to the amazing Raquel Pelzel for the nights of writing, editing, calls, and making sure I didn't go ova-board! Miss Lori Powell, you are truly amazing; thank you for such flawless food styling and recipe testing. To Natasha Louise King, who singlehandedly helped me style this book; your heart is so big, your wisdom is timeless, and your friendship has been vital, love you. Lola Volo, the world's best photo assistant, thank you and Mer-Shervolowood! Shannon, my talented and amazing friend. Adeena, Brit, Hannah, and Johnny, thank you from the bottom of my heart!

Team Rodale! Kara, thanks for the gorgeous graphics, lady! Aly, Olivia, Tory, Nancy, JoAnn, Yelena, Sasha, Jon, thank you for the countless time spent on this book, all of the support, edits, love, and heart. I am forever grateful for my first!

Dream Team WME: Justin, Kirby, Wachs, Bider, Amir, Rosen, Strand, Sherm,

Pyatt, Mullet, Warner. I have *never* been taken care of the way that you've all taken care of me. Thank you for being simply the best. Justin, you're my sunshine, I ruve you, truly thank you for every day. Kirby Kim, huge props, we did it, our book, thanks to you, dude! Wachs and Bides, NY loveys! Amir and Sherm, LA is where my heart will always be! Strand, you branding genius you!

I couldn't live a day without my girls, Steph, Andy, Christina, Casey, Tina, Suz, Courts, Becc, and Megs. Each one of you is so special and dear to my heart, and I am forever grateful for our friendship. Gwiazdowski family, love you all! Alexis, Fab, Tanis, Joey, Meesh and StyleCaster, Carly Harill, Mma Denise, love and thanks for the endless support. Kim Barnouin, love you, my friend. DJ Martinez, VA MiHigh luv! Mune and Karin-Team Glam-squad! Amanda and Eliz, Team PR adore! Ryan, luv u. Thank you, Mister Marc Duron @ABC Home NYC, A Loft Studios, Fishs Eddy, Team Vans, Chef Rob Wilson, Cynthia Sestiito, my culinary mentors. Life Coach, Todd Newton and Nan Colgan.

Mister Big Man Upstairs, I ask, you deliver . . . thank you for blessing me, I am so very grateful. My every day is dedicated to you. Word up yo xx.

Index

Underscored page references indicate boxed text. **Boldfaced** page references indicate photographs.